Dear Tina &
Happy New Year
All our best wishes for 2002
Bahar-Cemil, Hüso, Umeet

Nothing But
Time

Nothing But Time

A Woman's Struggle With Guillain-Barre Syndrome

☙❧

JUDY LIGHT AYYILDIZ

6-AYYI

revival story in chapter two first published as "Gathered At The Throne,"
2nd place winner, Piedmont Literary Review, Summer 1993

excerpt in chapter four from story first published as "Sour Cherries,"
Potato Eyes, Spring 1991

excerpts in chapters Five, Eight and Ten adapted from poetry in *Mud
River*, Lintel Press 1988: "Two-Minute Triumph," "Paper Dolls," and
"Gracie"

excerpt in chapter from "Early Morning In Zakopane," *Smuggled Seeds*,
Gusto Press

excerpt in the Afterwards adapted from "Last Walk With My Mother," The
Contemplative Way, Vol. 1, No. 2, Winter 1996

ORIGINAL COVER DESIGN, A PAINTING BY VEDII AYYILDIZ
PHOTO BY VEDII AYYILDIZ

This book was printed in the United States of America.

To order additional copies of this book, contact:
Xlibris Corporation
1-888-7-XLIBRIS
www.Xlibris.com
Orders@Xlibris.com

Contents

Dedication

For my mother, Laura Gladys Perry Light, who had
more courage than fear.

Also by JUDY LIGHT AYYILDIZ

co-authored with Rebekah Woodie:
The Writer's Express, creative writing lessons, Instructional Fair 1999
Easy Ideas For Busy Teachers, critical thinking,
Frank Schaffer Publications 1996
Creative Writing Across the Curriculum,
Frank Schaffer Publications 1995
Skyhooks and Grasshopper Traps, A Notebook of Poetry Lessons,
Skyhooks Pub. 1987

Mud River, poetry, Lintel Press 1988, 2nd ed. 1994
Smuggled Seeds, poetry, Gusto Press Series Winner 1979
First Recital, poetry chapbook, Leisure Publishing Co. 1977

FOREWARD

When the flood washes over both at dusk and dawn,
float on the dank waters, let go at the falls
where dragonflies dart in the arms of the sun.
Open to the gossiping wet tongues of the hills
—such tales of brick roads, primroses, and shale,
warm rain in the cool limbs of iridescent trees,
fans of white butterflies dusting a footbridge, or
drunken gnats serenading the wide-rimmed sombrero
of a lamp they once knew.

JLA

THANKS

Vedii–who will always stand by my side in the steps I take;

Kent, Kevin Kamal, and Karen who will understand my metaphor: *So deep, no wonder it's called a stairwell;*

the many nurses and therapists (whose names were changed to provide privacy) who helped me–most especially, Margaret; and Doctors: Gene A. Godwin, James Miller, and Donald B. Nolan;

The VCCA, AND Amanda Cockrell, Kamal Ayyildiz, Liz Jones, Rebekah Woodie, Jack Hatfield, Simone Poirier-Bures, Ken Taub, and Katie Letcher Lyle, who read drafts and made supportive suggestions, and last but never least, my daughter, Karen P. Ayyildiz, who did copyediting.

1

Neuro-Intensive Care

Sunday, 1 AM, July 6, 1985

I am still awake. Half of me can't move. Trapped in this bed, I stare up at spider-web cracks in the plaster, splintered lines like strings of nerves.

An eerie violence creeps through my body. Like a guerrilla army. It has ambushed, captured my nerve-system.

The doctors mention blood plasma transplant. Then say they're not sure it helps. Would my blood be removed, altered, and put back? They speak in their calm, professional voice so I'll feel safe.

Like when Dr. Miller brought up respiratory failure. Heart and lungs have nerves too. He's ready to put me on a respirator. What if I get to the place where I can't breathe? Is this paralysis permanent? If it gets worse, will I be able to talk? Could I go into a coma? Die?

Thirty-nine hours ago I walked up the hill to my house. Fourth of July fireworks shattered against the night sky. Less than a day later I'm hooked to machines. The one time it would be handy to have a husband who is a doctor, he's in Turkey.

The guy in the bed on the right side of me is almost gone. I hear them whisper as they work on his body:

"Had a stroke two weeks ago. No change yet."

Whispering, as if he could hear. He and the woman on the other side of me don't ever wake. I don't sleep. I can't raise up. My brain is juiced up. Like these florescent lights that stay on all the time. My mind jumps from one image to the next like some high-energy drug propels my thoughts, though they haven't even given me an aspirin.

The wall clock rules this space. Calls the doctor, regulates the nurses' methodical brush from beds, to desk, to door, floating white caps checking our radiant vital signs, angels with charts.

A gray-haired nurse has worked evening into night on the old man. Up-dating, mixing, injecting measured units of hope. When he inhales, it's a wobbling tone, a bass violin being tuned. His exhales whap. String breaks. He drones on and on.

The woman's jaw flutters when she breathes. Gives me The Willies. From the desk I heard,

". . . and brain tumor."

I eavesdrop on their pity. They can't operate. Her feathery rasp could be a bat flapping out of a cave. Must always be night wherever she is. If she's having an out-of-the-body experience, she knows I'm spying.

I must stay conscious. This paralysis moved in on me last night while I slept. My legs seem attached to my torso like dead-weight, rolls of sausage. My toes tent the sheets like a pyramid.

Yesterday, my thirteen year-old Karen stood in the driveway when the attendant wheeled me to the ambulance. Her eyes, wide as a spooked cat. She looked like an abandoned waif the way her jaw was clinched and one arm was holding the other. I was leaning back off the litter as they carted me away telling her not to worry I'd be fine.

I hear the rustling of Linda's starched uniform before I see her. Black curls trickle from her cap. Cherry lipstick shines. Lips pucker like some Forties' movie star. She hums, "Amazing Grace."

Linda sees me staring and stops mid-song, casually pulling her hands behind her back. I note the yellow blotch on her lapel that was not there thirty minutes ago and guess she had a sandwich with mustard. She smiles, studies the monitor, then looks down at me. "Hi," she says.

I mumble back.

"Who are you, my friend?" she asks.

I take a deep breath. They know who I am. I scrunch my lips like hers then answer, "Judy."

"Where are you?" She is shaking a finger.

I cross my arms, carefully. The pull of the IV throbs. She is waiting. "OK, Judy."

I am judging her restraint. The same round of questioning, every half hour since five o'clock last evening.

"We have to chart your physical and mental responses, " she repeats.

I give up. "I'm in the NICU, University Medical Center, Charlottesville, Virginia."

I like Linda. We've talked. We're both from West Virginia. She adjusts my pillow. "Do you know what day it is now?"

I lift my hands to let her smooth out the top of my sheet.

"Sunday. Yesterday was Saturday, tomorrow is Monday. This drill is irritating." She looks at me like I'm a spoiled second grader. I'm being naughty.

"You guys sure provide a hell of a night out on the town," I add.

Linda steps back, folds her arms, and trains that schoolmarm eye on me.

Green-eyed Sally brings me the bedpan. She never stops chattering with the two interns, who rattle off questions to me while they once again probe and tap my arms and legs.

The three of them lift me like a piece of furniture, slide the porcelain pan under my butt, and pull the sheet back up to my neck. My toilet.

Then, as if it is an outhouse with a door and sides, they stand waiting and talking as if I am not even here.

The hefty intern is asking Sally a question. "Did you try that new pineapple cheesecake down at the snack bar?"

Green-eyes licks her lips. "It's fantastic!"

Now the shapely female intern wants to know, "Is it real or frozen?"

It is like we are at a bus stop. I don't know where to look. Am I supposed to be a part of the group or invisible? I close my eyes and pretend I am a telephone pole.

I can't tell if anything is doing until the odor mingles with astringents and talcum.

Opening my eyes, I glance around. They don't even act as if they have noses. Momentarily, I move my shoulders and say, "OK."

The intern keeps talking as Sally pulls back the sheets. She coos like she's found a chocolate Easter egg.

"Oh, see what we have!"

Is it a compliment? Should I answer? It could be worse. I could be getting soapy enemas.

The lower half of me seems as if it's vanished, except for a deep heaviness. My legs are cool concrete. But I could feel that burning cold of the bedpan rim.

Beyond the pea green tent over my toes, 1:30 AM glares from the black-clawed clock. I shut my eyes and the clock leers from behind my lids. Time feels suspended, but those claws move from digit to digit, number and number, every second a nervous twitch, round and round. If I had a rubber arm I could take care of that clock.

Will I see my kids again? My husband, my mother?

Don't begin imagining Mother seeing me here.

Closing my eyes again, I force myself to see phosphorescent colors encircling my toes, blue-green energy spiraling my legs, curling up until I'm cocooned in colors and healing lights. I imagine gathering hundreds of sparkles of golds and greens and sucking them to my lungs. The sparkles are healing energy, flashing warriors now charging throughout my system.

It must be time for my husband to board his plane back from Istanbul. And he hasn't a clue what's going on with me. I'm glad I wouldn't let them call him. What could he do but worry the whole flight home?

Two weeks ago, Karen and I were on our way to California. Our mother-daughter adventure. Not that it turned out that well. I expected too much. Yeah, so I didn't plan it quite right, like the ritzy hotel in San Diego when we should have taken one on the beach where she would have met some teen types.

Maybe we should have gone to Turkey with her father after all. But what if I had awakened paralyzed in some Anatolian village? If the doctors at this university center know so little about my condition, what would doctors know on the Asian plains?

Time holds the answers. Negative draws negative. Focus on positive.

As a child, little did I know that using my imagination as a way to cope with my out-of-control world was practice for being a writer. When you're in a dark place, look up.

It's always darkest before the dawn.

Now, I'm really in a pit. The NICU. The nurse said that most patients in here rarely care how long the night gets, said my talking is a novelty.

I strain to listen past the doorway. The hallways out there are a tunneled maze. Ever so often, I hear laughter. It seems to flare up like a whirlwind. The maze must be full of cackles and croons and clangs. Stainless steel falling against the tile would toll like a bell. All over this hospital there must be machines gasping and sputtering. Sudden legs racing to keep up with the clock. Blithe spirits in white cotton soft-sole shuffling back and forth on their trained feet. And people standing up and walking off without having to think of telling their legs to move, their legs carrying their bodies like magic.

I can't believe I'm here. Yesterday afternoon the ambulance rushed up the Interstate from Roanoke to Charlottesville. Then I was on the litter in a corner of the emergency room somewhere downstairs.

The old nurse pattered up to me. She looked burnt-out, probably from years of overwork. She methodically took my pulse and temperature, jotted it on scrap paper and pinned it to my pillow with a safety pin.

"What's your problem?"

"Don't know, just can't move my legs."

She looked at me a few seconds. "Did you fall?"

"No."

She took a step back. "Well, did you lift something? Do you have any pain?"

When I said, "Not really," she decided I wasn't urgent. I saw the look. How many times I've heard a nurse or doctor's story about hypochondriac patients. I felt baffled and a bit embarrassed about my whole situation.

"Stay put and we'll get to you soon as we can." She nodded, then shunted off down the hall toward some commotion.

I was there for an hour. I suppose my chart got laid aside or overlooked in the circus of stab wounds and overdoses. I just laid there like a dummy, not making a fuss. There seemed to be so many coming in down the hall who were really sick. Years of being a doctor's wife didn't do a thing for me.

After their dinner, my life-saving crew came back to pick up their litter. Were they surprised. One of them gave me his big paper cup of *Hardee's* orange juice. I told him my heart was beginning to skip a few low-sugar beats. I crunched the ice between my teeth as the driver went for help. I heard him arguing. They found my chart, and suddenly I got lots of attention from those five nervous residents from neurology. They had been waiting. "For over an hour!" one of them claimed. As if I had been the one playing hooky.

I pride myself on having an inquiring mind. I should have realized from the very onset of the numbness that it was steadily creeping up. Am I neglectful or dense? Some force was taking control of my body bit by bit. Why didn't I comprehend that? Responsibilities? I can't be an emergency? Because I am a mother? Ha! Welcome, Ego, to the Time-Out Zone.

My nurses bathe and dress me skillfully as undertakers. When they're bored, I get massaged. Since I can't sit, they fluff my linens, feed me broth. I tell jokes, anything to distract, tales about my childhood, my three kids, can't seem to stop talking, whether aloud or in my mind. Can't let myself fall into the black hole. I got paralyzed in my sleep.

Linda is patting my arm. I smile back like she is right.

". . . even though you tell a lot of stories—"

Is she hinting that my stories are getting on her nerves? The IV aches like an impacted tooth. I make a fist with the other hand, raise my arm and bend my elbow.

"My arms are still working fine, see?"

"I see, and yes you look good. Anything you need?"

I could give Linda a list, but I answer her in a nice southern voice.

"Not a thing right at this moment."

"Fine and dandy."

Linda turns, takes three steps over to the white desk under the clock, writes on my chart, replaces the chart in its slot and she's out the door.

OK, I'll just close my lids, won't go to sleep, will try to relax, do a deadman's float on a wide, placid river,—going where, it doesn't matter.

Scenes from the last three days begin to pass in my mind like a movie reel: Friday, almost two days ago, July 4th. I am bouncing around, shopping for furniture, fresh tomatoes, beans and corn from the Farmers' Market.

After I come home, I am cooking for the street party this evening, then climbing up into the attic over the garage to get the metal table for the picnic. Do I strain my back? No, no pain. I lug the table to the opening at the steps, lean against the railing, ease it over a bit, then step down backwards.

Is there an answer for me in that garage? Concentrate. Did I hurt my back when I carried that table down that ladder in the garage? My limbs are on the thin side. But they're wiry, strong. I learned back in West Virginia the proper way to lift heavy objects.

When my boys were small I moved a piano out the front door, around the hill and down to the rec. room. I was 120 pounds then, before my baby girl was born. The old man next door stood on the hill and watched me for the hour and half it took me to do it.

Yard by yard, with rugs, ropes, and boards, I lugged that spinet around the house and in through the French doors at the back. I was determined to show my darling husband, Vedi, I'd get that piano moved downstairs in spite of his saying we didn't need to have a moving company out, that the piano served as a perfectly good piece of furniture in the living room. But it was mine and I wanted it to be where I wanted it to be. Nobody played it but me. He said, "Leave it until we can get a couch."

I finally got it down the bank by using the big oak tree on the side as leverage. The old man had been standing all that time in his flower garden, watching.

When I finished, he spoke. "Little girl, I never saw anything like that in my life. Must be because you are a redhead." People always think red-heads are gutsy. If it's not that, it's the freckles. I tell them it's really because I'm an independent-minded Scotch-Irish poet. Seeing Vedi's surprised face that evening was worth the effort. More ways to skin a cat than one.

Rewind. Friday, yes, an active day with no signs of illness, not even throughout Friday evening as I climb the hill with neighbors to watch fireworks explode over Roanoke. All the neighborhood kids had run ahead. We amble around the bend, and up the grade. A breeze dries the sweat from my neck. On the knoll, we sip drinks. Celebrations. Wildflowers bursting above layers of purpled mountains. I sit, bathed in the artificial glow from below and the star shine overhead. It's cool and serene.

"Mom, can I spend the night with Missy?"

"Sure, Karen, if her mom says so."

"You don't mind staying alone tonight?"

"No, Honey. Go ahead. I'd best enjoy the quiet. Those two brothers of yours will be home from camping Monday."

"And Dad comes home Sunday, right?"

"Yes, Vedi will come with a trunk full of presents, maybe those exotic earrings."

"And lots of pictures of our Turkish relatives."

Karen's reply had made me miss Vedi's mother, and I knew she would tuck a treasure for me into his luggage. But he'll be glad to get back. When he's in the states, Istanbulian memories take on a romantic luster. When he gets over there, he longs for the Blue Ridge.

The clock says 3:45 AM. He'll land in eight hours. Life will get back to normal. When he phones home, they'll tell him where to find me.

5:45 AM.

Did I do something to make myself paralyzed? When Kevin and Kent were small, if they got hurt, I felt responsible. There's no reason I should feel guilty for being ill. Yet something nags at me, saying,

"Oh yes, but you're always doing too much, never content. Now you've made yourself sick."

That's Mother's voice. I can see Mother standing in some doorway with tears in her blue eyes, looking hurt and scared, having lived her whole life fearing the unknown and what the neighbors think. She stayed with Daddy all those years when he drank. Dad was the indisputable head. We didn't share personal feelings much and never let outsiders know what was going on inside.

"You just have to get through hard times the best you can then forget it," Mother said.

She said that over and over. Yet, I've learned that not only do you have to dig up the past, you have to sort through it like an archeologist.

My father certainly wasn't accepting of Vedi like Vedi's mother was of me. Daddy was in the habit of refusing my beaus. Vedi's being a foreigner was a good an excuse as any. I thought in time Daddy would relent. But his time stopped.

He died in a hospital bed still not speaking to me.

Daddy, you've been gone a long time now. We had our problems, but you taught me how to see with the eyes of a poet. Called me out with you under a cold night sky saying,

"Look how she twinkles messages. That's Venus, my birth star."

Oh, you were some story teller. You showed me how to look at things from a different angle–like that December when I was thirteen.

Daddy took us kids to pick out a tree. The plan was to have it up and decorated by the time he brought Mamma home from waitressing at Jim's Grill and Spaghetti House. It was a white Christmassy day, fluffy snow banked up against the curbs, hooded on the cars, and glinting with red and green from the decorations strung over the village of Barboursville.

"We'll get a bargain here. They'll try to gyp you down in Huntington," Daddy was saying as we piled out of the whale-finned Plymouth.

The farmers sold trees off the back of their pickups. It was about four-thirty. The wind was kicking up a bit and some sagging dark clouds back over the hills to the north were promising more snow. The next day was the last before vacation. Jon was betting there would be no school. He had asked if he could stay out late sledding with the guys. "Yes, but we have to get this damn tree first or your Mother will have a fit," Daddy answered.

We knew Daddy was the one who wanted to get the tree bought, that he had most likely finished with his shopping; and as soon as the tree was up and all was set for Christmas, he could begin celebrating the holidays. That meant nipping at Jack Daniel's until New Year's Day, when he would bite the bullet, sober up and go back to selling Kirby sweepers.

Little Pete had already climbed up in the garage and hauled down the dog-eared boxes of scratched glass bulbs, frayed gold tinsel, two cords of lights and a silver star with the center missing. But, we would spruce-up the star by draping angel hair around it. Each year, we added something new to our decorations, usually whatever Sears had on sale. The previous year we had gotten a can of aerosol snow that stuck like paint to the window frames. It was near Easter before we got it all off. We knew better than to mention that stuff again. This year, we had a string of fingernail-sized blinking lights from Japan.

We had come to Main Street to buy the tree. Actually, there was only one main street, and on its corner sat the S. & H. Grill, with the "Ten-cent Store" across the street, the post office round the corner and the high school and football field a quarter of a mile on. New flakes started to spit and we felt reckless as fleas on a skunk.

Our living room wouldn't accommodate a large tree, so we were obliged to get one that was not too full. However, our ceiling was a cathedral with rafters; so we could get a tall one.

Pete squealed, "Get that one there. If you cut off the bottom part, you won't see the hole!"

But Daddy didn't want to do any sawing off ends this evening because the dark was moving in fast. He wanted that tree up and done with when he brought Mamma home. Jon found one, twirled it around and we all speculated it was nifty; but the farmer wanted five bucks for it.

"Tell you what," Daddy began, knowing the guy wanted to get rid of us so he could take a dinner break, "It's scrawny, but the kids like it; so I'll give you four and a quarter." Daddy had already calculated he would settle for the four-fifty. We lugged the pine across the street and stuck it into the wide trunk of the car.

On the way home, we dropped off Jon. Pete had begged to tag along.

Daddy told them, "Go on, boys have to be boys, but you better not go hitching any rides on the bumpers of any more cars or it will be the last time you will sit till Groundhog's Day."

Daddy eased the car on around Pea Ridge Road in the hoary dusk, fighting snow with the windshield wipers. We parked at the bottom of the steep drive because the car might not make it back down in two hours when it was time to go after Mamma. The two of us wrestled the tree up the bank and down the walk to the porch.

While Daddy nailed a stubby cross to the base of the pine, I got the washtub and filled it with water. We would set that tree down in the water, throw a sheet over the tub and feel fire-safe for two weeks.

It wasn't long before Daddy lugged the tree into the living room. He began hoisting it, bottom-up and over. He paused and turned to me. Immediately, I saw that we were experiencing a mutual brainstorm. Simultaneously, we glanced to the rafter and back to each other.

"Do you think we should do it?" he asked, brown eyes brimming with the image. He raised the cross-bottomed fir up against the beam. I studied the picture.

"Over a bit to the right. Yeah. That's perfect." I added, intending to put the studied measurement of a professional in my voice.

That was all the encouragement the man needed. I climbed up on a chair and steadied the trunk while he tied it to the rafter.

We stood back and accessed our deed. Daddy grinned.

"Why, your mom ought to like this. We can walk all around it. We'll just stack the presents under the star."

In an hour, the tree was decorated and we were bragging to ourselves on our ingenuity and originality, completely forgetting that his wife and my Mamma is Scotch, having one of the hardest streaks of the conventional that ever came down the pike. She sure would be tickled pink, we agreed. How could she be anything but glad, with it all decked out–or Up, so to speak, and glowing above us like a shrine? It would be like when we gave her the Mother's Day bird. She might even cry.

By the time we got Mamma back, Daddy was forced to park way out on Mayhood Road; and we had to trudge on around the gravel road, up the drive and down the slippery walk to the house. Daddy and I hadn't told her about the surprise.

Mamma was tired and in no festive mood. The radio we left on in the kitchen was extolling winter wonderlands. We announced the tree ready for inspection. She answered flatly.

"Well, all I want to do is sit and watch those new blinking lights–with my feet up."

We couldn't wait to see her face when she spied the sight. I moved around the corner of the door and switched on the tree's lights. She shut her eyes and I led her into the room.

Sure enough, then she opened them, she stared a few seconds, then started to cry. Daddy winked at me and nodded. She likes it, we said through our exchanged glances. Right?

But, wrong, she didn't like it. She snarled at us.

"Whoever in their right mind heard of a Christmas tree hanging from a rafter?"

She went on to say she couldn't depend on the two of us doing anything sensible. Mamma thought it was a bad joke. She told us in no uncertain terms that she was not going to have a foolish Christmas, that she was going into the kitchen to get a snack and then she was going to bed and when she awoke the following morning, our tree had better be sitting on the floor where it belonged. She meant it.

We were fond of our creation, but there was no way either of us had the guts to challenge her on this one. So, we undressed it, took it down, and set it up–in an acceptable position.

Daddy wrote a poem the next day, a take-off on, "The Night Before Christmas," with lines in it like:

The Christmas tree hung on the rafter above,
And would swing back and forth if you gave it a shove.

When the boys got in, they laughed all the while they helped us re-decorate, while Mamma slept. They thought the upside-down Christmas tree was a great idea too. Daddy started his Christmas nipping. By the next morning, we were snowed-in tight as a jug, with an extra day of vacation from school.

One morning a couple of years ago, I was leafing through magazines before hauling them to be recycled, and this full-page photo caught my eye: A glistening Christmas tree hung from a rafter, its big silver star shining down on the presents stacked on the floor beneath it. Seems this highfalutin decorator created quite a reputation for himself with his innovative idea. Guess most conceptions depend on point of view. The idea still seems pretty nifty to me.

That moment two nights ago is stuck in my mind: 11:00 PM, after the fireworks, standing at my bedroom closet looking down at my tennis shoes, no socks. I didn't untie them but balanced on the right foot while my hand steadied against the wall as I pushed the heel with the toe of the left.

My right foot pulled up but the shoe seemed to want to suck it back. I kicked away the right shoe then the left, paused to rub my soles against the carpet and noticed a tingling on the bottoms of my feet, which I figured was from running around all day in tennis shoes.

Later, a dream: Exhausted me was trying to take an inventory of a huge warehouse but couldn't get my legs to move down the aisles fast enough and I seemed to be running out of time. I awoke in a sweat, threw back the covers and sat on the side of the bed. 2:00 AM. Had to pee.

I stumbled, caught myself against the night stand. My feet must have gone to sleep. No wonder the dream. Went to the bathroom unsteadily then back to bed.

Next, it was 6:00 AM. Slung first one leg then the other over the side of the bed. When I put my weight on my legs, I collapsed to the floor.

Shocked, I sat there with a pang of memory: my feet last night. What was going on? I rubbed my soles on the carpet, pinched my calves, then tried to get up by pulling on the mattress; but my legs wouldn't cooperate.

I crawled to the desk. My arms couldn't lift my body. I slipped, hit my shoulder. No strength in my lower legs. Impossible. Mind tricks? Nothing like this had ever happened to me. I had to get moving. Lying on my side, I lugged my hips and legs, elbows skinning against the carpet.

Finally I was in the bathroom wrestling with the commode. No way could I pull my hips up onto the seat. After ten minutes, my belly was stretched across the top. I dangled, figuring how to turn over and straighten up. The water beneath my abdomen was cool but I was stranded in my heaviness.

My hips thudded against the tile when I let my weight pull me from the commode. Anger, big tears and a howl didn't help. I imagined amused powers watching me and yelled at them.

"O.K., this is enough!"

No response.

"I won't give in. I have to go, but I will NOT pee on the floor!" The air signed from the floor vents.

I hauled weight to the bathtub, grabbed the water spout with my right hand and pushed against the side with the left until the top half of me was juggled onto the rim of the tub. I yanked at my right leg until it was up and over. Inch by inch, I lowered my body inside.

Pulling myself into sitting was easy but turning to face the spout was another matter. My arms were cranes, lifting and positioning, first the left leg then the right as I pivoted on my tailbone. Grunting and heaving for breath, I wrenched my nightgown from under my butt, then rolled it and held it up with my chin while I turned on the water. Splashing my abdomen, I relieved my bladder. Maybe the water would revive me.

When I shut off the water I sat in a chill. My legs were still lifeless, and now my nightgown was wet. The thought of what it would take to get dressed was overwhelming.

My heart was racing. The clock by the sink told me a whole hour had gone by. I dug back out over the tub, letting upper torso pull the lower.

Yanking a towel from a rung on the wall, I dried off, taking account of the sore places on my body. They would be bruises. My elbows were near bleeding.

When I saw that the skin on the top of my feet was scraped raw, a realization creamed over me: I hadn't been feeling the damage to my feet. Sitting there in a damp nightgown pondering wouldn't solve anything. Move! Scrunching and wiggling like a snail got me to the bedroom.

The waterbed stretched before me like a plateau that I desperately wanted. Back in bed, I could figure out how to handle this attack of whatever it was. The challenge was to get up there.

I grabbed the bottom of the desk chair and tugged it to the bed, then pulled and heaved until my torso was belly-down across its armless seat.

I rolled over onto the bobbing bed. The warm softness of the covers soaked my skin like lotion.

Thoughts had to get organized, self gotten together. There had to be some way for me to comprehend this nonsense. Calm, I had to steady my breathing, steadily, like I was pulling a cord to slow a train.

I concentrated on an image of a peaceful surface, a mountain lake shimmering in a coral sunset, where I forced myself to glide into the center. The engine in my chest slowed.

Gradually the reality of my situation came clear: PARALYSIS. My body went to sleep last night and my legs didn't wake up.

Oh, my dear spirit, help my body.

I opened my eyes. My mind threatened panic. Take it easy, take stock of what is happening. I analyzed: no sickness or pain. Could I have had a stroke? Would not a brain tumor present signs? Of the last few days and weeks, there had been no hint of blurred vision, dizziness or lack of coordination. Certainly I had never heard of sudden paralysis coming on anyone without a reason.

Maybe I'm just losing my marbles. I should dial 911. No, I'll wait for Karen.

I kept checking to see if I could wiggle my toes.

I can't do it yet but this might go away any minute.

The doorbell began dinging like an ice cream truck. 9:05 AM. Karen. I knew she'd be shaking her short crop of dark brown hair, thinking I was sleeping, wishing she'd taken her key.

I flung the back the covers. My legs wouldn't move. Pulling with my upper torso I rolled the lower. Hips might as well have been a lump of iron. I juggled myself to the edge of the bed, flopped onto the chair, pushed it away, then spilled backwards onto the floor, breaking my fall with an arm. My breath came in heaves. The numbness was getting into my thighs.

Dragging my body, elbows like a seal climbing over rocks on its way to the sea, I finned out the hall, sprawling halfway with my damp nightgown balled up around my chest.

Giggles slid through the door, into the hall. Missy was with Karen. I took a gulp of air and thrashed toward the foyer. Karen's calling reverberated in my throat while I stretched and slithered on the cool tile to the door.

They were peeking though the side window. What would the girls think when they saw me? What would I say? The bell rang again. I reached up, grasped the lock and hitched it back.

An hour later, Dr. Gene, our friend and GP for years, was on his way to my house. Determined to block out terrible thoughts, I told myself,

Now everything will be all right.

But white light terror inside me kept exploding, expanding.

I have to somehow contain it! If I don't, it will burn me to cinders. Control. Must have control. Use thought-forms.

In my mind, I invented a small metal box on a distant shelf, opened its lid, blew the pulsating silver-white terror inside it, shut the lid, turned the key, and walk away from it. Walked away.

11:00 AM

Can it be only yesterday morning I was in my own bed, in my own gown? What am I doing now? Making a sore place on my lip. Biting my lip and pinching my arm to make sure I can still feel pain. Squeeze my thigh—nothing. My mind keeps swirl with remembering: There, in my bedroom, where my old friend and doctor came, there where I first lay in the eye of this tornado that began to gather with it the essentials of my life, taking me down a rabbit's hole, depositing me here, from where all in the matter of a bit more than an hour's time I went from hearing Gene Godwin say he thought I have something, it sounded like he said, Green Beret—then, to an examination on the carpet of my bedroom floor with Dr. Nolan, a neurologist, who seemed to confirm, and they were talking in waves, splashing in the air around my space, calling an ambulance, considering whether to phone Vedi, me, saying, Why disturb his mind all the way across the Atlantic, he will leave Turkey in a few hours. No. No need to disturb him, when he gets home, everything will be proven just a big mistake, why are we getting ready to go to Charlottesville, why are neighbors around, helping me collect my things, myself, women who are neighbors, not close friends, picking up my lotions, shampoo, slippers, bringing them to put in a small suitcase, it all seems so silly, I'll be back before nightfall, they, wheeling me around on my desk chair, joking how convenient to have a chair with wheels handy, and then me insisting to put on make-up, don't want to look sick, in the middle of this rush on a floating stage where I seem to have a leading role but no power over anything, trying to act as if this were somehow all normal, wanting them to go home, let me escape back to my bed, but I am unable to put anything in motion, I am the one acted upon, they are all so efficient, all those strangers taking over my home, where I am dislocated, unhinged, wishing the house were in better order for their probing eyes and hands, wondering why there is a discussion of getting a helicopter, wondering why the anxiety, wondering if it is because I am a doctor's wife getting too much attention, telling myself, I shouldn't have these thoughts, and then, I was lifted, placed on a litter, carted out the front door, down the walk,–yes, neighbors gathered to watch me leave, I tried to read their lips, decipher the way they stood in groups of two and three, whispering, I was hoisted up and shoved inside the back door of the ambulance, my litter locked into the side, strap clicked around my waist, the double doors shut, I felt the bump of the driveway, as the siren started, inside a moving box, strained to see out the back window, watched the rock wall smearing back into the distance, then, for two hours, exhaust fumes seeping through the back doors, talking with the attendant who alternately wiped his head then mine, took my pulse, asked me, *How's your breathing, How are you feeling now, is your swallowing still OK?* and all I could say was *Fine, I'm fine* and wondered what was all this rush, this rush down I-81, passing towering two-ton trucks with a freight-train roar, going God knows how fast, swerving to the left and swinging back to the right–, but I was not fine, still couldn't move my lower half, a bit nauseated from the speed and fumes, clutched the handle above my head, kept having thoughts that the litter might break loose and crash through the two back doors, send me spinning out at break-neck speed on the highway under the grinding tires of the trucks, squashed beyond recognition like the possums that come down to the roads in spring, the ones that never get across, the ones that survive only as bits of ragged fur, splotched like warm pouches of raspberries, stuck fast on the concrete, head and eyes spread in an indistinguishable mass at once with the tires and gush of noise, I thought, *All this must be a bizarre dream from which I am bound to wake,* yet pain from a cramp knotted in my leg brought me to know it couldn't be a dream—I had seen pain, but never felt the fist of pain so intensely as I did, the attendant with the heavy hands and big face full of wrinkles gathering into a reassuring smile massaging my leg saying, *Take it easy, take it easy, we'll be there soon, Are you having trouble breathing, Are you all right?* and the sound of the tornado shoved the cars around our moving box, one at a time, they wheezed, *all right . . . all right . . . all right.*

2:00 PM

Two hours ago, they read me that note.

Your brother, Pete, your mother and Aunt Pauline are on their way from Huntington.

Who told them? Mother will be frantic. They should be here soon. It's a six hour's drive. Vedi should be landing at Kennedy. He'll phone home, they'll tell him.

What will they tell him?

We'll get through this. Life isn't always meant to be easy. We've had hurdles before.

It was the summer I was nineteen. No one home but me and Daddy, Mamma working. I had come home to find him waiting.

"Where have you been?"

I knew he already knew, he always found out. "Over at the Stone Lodge pool with Rosie."

He moved toward me like a bull. "Rosie, ha—you've been at that motel with the Native! Try to raise you right, you a Sunday school teacher, some church girl you are, hanging out in a motel–"

I flushed with anger at that word he used for the young man I had loved for two years. Daddy's stories had betrayed me, how he always had bragged about his great-great grandmamma's being a full-blooded Cherokee, and when I had come home from 4-H camp telling him I had a boyfriend who was part Native American, he raged and forbid.

"That was a tale, our family doesn't have any mixed blood!"

But this was my first love, this was forever, and my love was the most beautiful thing I had ever known and I would not give him up, saw him at ball games, at school, with friends. And that day I had spent two hours sitting with him and my friend at the side of a pool.

"Our relationship is pure, we only–"

His big hand came down across my cheek. "You're no better than a whore!"

I turned with the force of his blow and ran out the door, off the screened-in back porch, across the yard and out into the woods. A thunderstorm had started about the time I had come home, and as I ran my tears washed into the rain, the rain slapping on my legs, my shorts and shirt soaking to my skin, my bare feet splashing over old leaves and brush. I stopped and stood in pouring rain and water to my ankles, looking up through the swaying tall trees, lightning and thunder all around me.

"God damn you, God!" The lightning flashed near by and the wind tore at the tops of the trees.

"Here I am! Why don't you just strike me dead?! I dare you! You give me something wonderful to love and then punish me for wanting it. What's to live for?"

I expected God to strike me there standing in the water in the middle of the storm. And I could care less, I was tired of fighting. But suddenly, as quickly as the storm had moved in and the torrents started, it was turned off like someone shutting off a shower. There were quickly only drops falling from the drooping trees.

Then, it happened: Something invisible poured over my head, slid down my shoulders, arms, legs and around my feet. Like warm oil it was, and soothing. I didn't hear a sound except a bird that had started, but it was as if God had let me know it would be all right.

I became calm and sure before I walked back home.

A year later, I would turn away from my heart's treasure because of Daddy's threats, but I somehow knew my life would be all right if I could just leave home.

Daddy didn't want to hear anything good about my Turk. "From now on I have no daughter." I had already left home that spring.

"Tell her she can come home when she gets the divorce."

I wasn't his possession any more. I was twenty-one and it was as if I had risen from the dead, a junior in the music department at Marshall University with a twenty-five dollar a week job at Anderson-Newcomb Department Store. My three roommates and I split everything, and I was able to make it. Tuition was about one hundred dollars a semester. I was an ecstatic spirit, an uncaged bird; and Vedi walked into that room where I was sitting, and started an April to November courtship to marriage that most of my friends and professors thought would never last.

You are from different backgrounds, cultures, religions. Physicians and artist-types won't mix. What if he wants to take you back to Turkey? What if he already has three wives? His family won't accept you. You are a South-ern Baptist.

But it was our differences that attracted us. And, the sweet smell of his skin, the way his hair curled on his forehead when he perspired, the mischievous light in his dark brown eyes.

Vedi was a romantic. He sat at the kitchen table in that little apartment of mine and read my fortune in late-night tea cups

"Oh, you are going to be a published poet," he said, grinning into his fat dimples.

I had never had a fortune read. I leaned my face across the yellow chrome table to look in the cup.

"I can't see where you can know that."

Vedi cocked his head and sat back.

"You have to trust me," he whispered.

There were free concerts in the summer air on the banks of the Ohio that we went to in a misty rain. "Moon River" became our song and Vedi named me his "Huckleberry Friend." Entranced by my new, unlimited world I floated carefree as Holly Golightly.

After I waited some evenings in his room for up to three hours while he did surgery, he would take me in through the back door of the hospital kitchen where we opened the refrigerators and heaped our plates with leftovers. Then he would listen to my latest song or poem and exclaim it, "A gem from the gods," squeezing my hand as if he believed it.

He made me believe. I was captivated by his deep and generous heart. He, too, was an artist, who carted his tubes of oils around in a wooden box, Van Gogh, his ideal.

"Sure my family will accept you," he insisted, when I gave reasons why we should not marry.

Then, his mother, Ana, wrote back that she had had a dream about her son marrying a school teacher in America—before she even received our letter. I was enchanted with her before I met her.

Two years later she came through the door of our apartment in Buffalo, New York with a big black handbag stuffed full of scarves and charms, along with cheeses, packets of sugar, and plastic spoons she kept from the airplane flight. Vedi followed, lugging a suitcase that looked as if it would burst its seam. It was stuffed with silver and carpets.

Kent was still crawling, and my heart was aching because I would have to leave him Monday when I began teaching. Vedi always left for work before dawn and returned at night long after dark. He only went across the street to his residency at Roswell Park Cancer Institute, but he might as well be miles away.

For Kent, I'd lined-up a curly-haired Irish woman who'd done "baby-minding" for years. In a thick brogue she repeated,

"Oh, God bless yer lettle hert!" and I hoped she really did love children and was a dedicated Catholic who would not let my baby out of her sight.

Vedi's mother wasn't with us more than a quarter of an hour when she put an end to the idea of any outsider taking care of her grandson. She spoke little English; but she knew how to say, "No, I take Kent, no woman."

She took care of all of us that year. I called her the Turkish, Ana–mother. It started snowing in October and didn't quit until April. I got home on week-days after the sun set. She always had Kent bathed and dressed.

Ana had me put my feet up while she brought me hot tea and freshly-made borek. She pampered me and flooded me with compliments. I adored her. Ana stayed with us that first time for a year and a half.

Is anything ever really finished? Daddy's gone and here I am in NICU between two half-dead people. I asked Daddy once if he was afraid of death. He didn't even look up, just kept playing at trying to beat what he called, "Old Sol"–solitaire, laying each card down with a delicate deliberation.

"I'd look death right in the eye and ask what took him so long." I was impressed.

It's ironic that the first time Vedi met Daddy was in the funeral home. Vedi stared at Daddy in his casket. It's also ironic that Vedi's ended up being Mother's best friend all these years.

You can die quickly, even in a hospital. The night Daddy died, the nurses didn't recognize the reason he was wandering into other people's rooms–heart failure. Brain lacked oxygen. They brought him back and strapped him down. They didn't even call his doctor.

When you die, do you know you've gone out of your body? All feelings just go blank? Would you try to get back into the body to revive it? Float around watching what they do to it? One day you're at the center of everything, people waiting for decisions, and the next, you're off in some far corner, so remote you can't see if you're missed or not.

Nurse Linda will be back in for more stories soon. I'll tell her one to make her laugh. Keeping the lid on that box.

3:30 PM

A twinge of alarm. Voices in the hall, West Virginia twang mixed in with my aunt's acquired Pittsburgh accent. My brother Pete, Mother, and Aunt Pauline are seconds away from coming through the door. Mother will fall apart when she sees me, and I won't be able to do a thing to help her.

I pretend sleep but open my eyes when I hear the pained and high-pitched, "Oh, Lordy, Lord—what are we going to do?!"

"Mother, it's all right."

Pauline clutches her elbow. Pete moves to Mother's other side. In seconds, she takes in the IV, the cords, the monitor. Her eyes become blue porcelain. She looks first to the bed on my right, then to the one on the left. I lean my head and shoulders forward as if I could catch my Mother when she faints.

"I can't stand it!" She moans.

Her hair has fallen cock-eyed over her brow. Head is shaking.

"Mother—listen! It's not as bad as it looks."

But she is swooning. The bleeps of the monitors seem to blare.

Then, as if they were waiting for the moment, two nurses appear. Pete and Pauline fall back as the nurses move to Mother's sides. She is crying as they take her from the room. I extend my hand toward the back of her hunched shoulders. It is trembling when I drop it to the sheet. Pauline reaches down and soothes her hand on mine. She speaks softly.

"After Karen called we couldn't stop her from coming, but she'll be fine after she gets over the shock."

"Vedi called from New York," Pete states, as if he were giving an up-dated weather report. "He changed his ticket. Is due here in about two hours."

I look at my tall, younger brother. His back is still straight from the twenty years he spent in the air force. He is tired but calmed, knows about handling situations. I've been to Korea, the Aleutian Chain, Vietnam and Minot, South Dakota twice, he likes to say. There are bags under his eyes, and the corners of his mouth are tucked tight under his cheeks, as if for leverage.

"Well, Sis, what in the hell have you done to yourself?" He is grinning. "You look like somebody's damn science project." Then he chuckles. I chuckle back.

"What can we do for you?" he asks, then adds without waiting for an answer, "We got a room at the motel down the street. Told Vedi to come there."

I look at him, then to Mother's younger sister. I have felt the warmth of her regard for the last few minutes. She hasn't taken her eyes off my face. I'm so glad she's with Mother, so grateful she cared enough to make the trip.

"Look Honey, I was in your position twenty years ago when my back gave out before I had surgery." Pauline squeezes my hand.

"Yes Ma'am, and I had pain too, but I just held on and knew I could make it, knew I would, by the grace of God, get on my feet, and look at me now, here for you. And looky here, Honey, your Mom'll brace up like she always does. She's a trooper. Not a one of my mom's eleven kids is a quitter. You're the same blood."

I reach out both hands. Pete comes around the bed and takes the other one. These kin offer me strength dug up out of the hills.

"What's that?" Pete asks, pointing to the pyramid at the foot of my bed. "When your legs went numb, did your feet start growing?"

I have Pauline pull the covers back off my legs.

"Doctor ordered me some foot braces made–to protect my ankles." They stare at the plastic molded to fit my feet and calves.

"They keep me straight," I add, "–as if I could go the wrong way right now."

Pete stuffs his hands into his blue jeans' pockets and stretches his shoulders toward my feet, surmising. "I'd say they made you some gladiator shoes." He shakes his head and chuckles.

"Well, you'll manage whatever it is," Pauline says, tight-lipped. She softens her lips into a smile. "I remember when you were born," she says.

"Mother and Daddy lived with Granny and Grampaw, didn't they?" Pete says.

"West Virginia was still in the Depression," Pauline says. "I used to come to the farm often. You were always a spunky kid. I liked that about you."

"Tell Pete your story about me cutting my hair," I say.

"Oh, lawh–why, a whole bunch of my sisters and brothers had come up to the Teays farm for the weekend." Pauline paused. "You haven't heard this one, Pete?"

He shrugs.

"Judy," Pauline says, "hated her pigtails. Snuck into the bedroom and whacked one off with mom's scissors and left it on the floor. Your mother saw it lying there and let out this whelp. Thought it was a snake got in the house, and your Grampaw came running with a hoe, with the rest of the clan on his heels. Lord, how we laughed."

"Just one pigtail?"

"Sure, Pete, and Gladys, your mother, had fixed Judy's hair in a French braid and Judy had whacked it at the root, so then Gladys had to cut it all short as your brother, Jon's."

"Aunt Pauline, tell him what I said when they asked me why I did it."

"Judy might have been only three but she was sly. Stood right in front of everybody and rolled her eyes and said, 'God told me to do it.'"

Pete glances over to me with raised eyebrows then back to Pauline. "Guess no one could fault her for doing the Lord's will."

Pauline's eyes crinkle up and dance into the lights of her glasses. I am soaking up their presence like a balm.

"Well, Aunt Pauline, all that happened before you married a steel mill boss and went off to Pittsburgh," I say.

"But I still love you," she answers, "and know you are still that spunky gal."

Pete crosses his arms and stares at me.

"I wonder how you ever caught this disease–they call it a syndrome? Maybe you just happened in onto the wrong place at the right time to get lambasted with this whatever-they-call-it syndrome."

I've carried the scar that looks like a slice of cantaloupe on the top of my left foot ever since the summer I was four and Jon was seven, when we lived in that two-story wooden house with a wrap-around porch.

In that same place, I remember being held down by Mamma on the swing that hung from its ceiling with chains and hooks, while Granny was forcing a tablespoon of caster oil into my mouth.

"This'll clean you out and keep you well." Granny's words.

I had the attitude that I was being punished, but inside I was pretty sure I had done something or other to come by it honest.

I probably felt the same way about getting just deserts a little over a year earlier, although I'm not sure, when my face swelled up like a pig, red and boiling, the day after I had caught myself on fire. Granny and Mamma had been in the back yard hanging out clothes and I was in the living room alone, rolling a page of newspaper into a long wand. I wanted to be like my Daddy, who was the final word on most all that went on with us, unless Granny decided to override him, like she did when he cut two long switches and set them up in the hall to remind us to be good. She made him throw those switches away.

Daddy smoked cigarettes, making pretty figures in the air with his breath. I would sit in fascination of his quiet magic. I figured I, too, could make images in the air; so, my imagination caught fire.

The outcome of that moment in time with me and the rolled newspaper on that cold spring day was that, everything considered, I was lucky to have been wearing a dress with a high neckline. Lucky that my long hair was in braids, and that I blew out on the burning wand instead of knowing to inhale.

There was more luck, too: It was washday.

When I caught on fire and began screaming, both mothers came running back into the house. Granny got there first and burned her hands trying to put me out, but Mama was fast on her heels with a bucket of water scooped up from the washtub which sat ready on the kitchen table.

They treated me with aspirin, lard and ice, and didn't call the doctor until the next day, after the swelling had come up over night.

The old doc said, "Couldn't have done much more if I'd have been here. You're sure fortunate, little lady."

Even though I've had plastic surgery, which has erased most of the evidence of that day, you can still see crumpled skin on the left side of my smile.

That house capped a knoll above a winding two-lane road. Granny's youngest living daughter, Odetta, used to do her courting beneath the gigantic oak that spread at the foot of the hill. Wilkie, her lover, had a blue Ford. Jon and I delighted in nothing better than to hide near the bushes while they kissed, her long blonde hair and his black making a curious valentine behind smoky glass.

At the foot of the rutted driveway, a large tree had been sawed down. Its stump became a cutting block. Daddy would split logs there with one mighty swing of the ax. Jon and I would crouch back up on the bank where we had been stationed out of the space of flying chips. It seemed to be the most wonderful thing in the world to be a grown-up—who could sit in cars and kiss in the sunset or split great trees into heaping teepees of sticks, which the two of us got to carry up to the house for Granny's biscuit oven or to feed the hungry fire in the living room.

Then, too, there was the time Jon and I got put out of the house on a cold January day because we kept coming into the room where either a brother or sister was trying to be born. We watched through the window and saw the doctor magically lift a baby out of a table, just as if it was a rabbit from a hat. I later was told how doctors brought their own tables for birthing in those days, folded up and carried like a suitcase.

Grampaw caught us peeking through the keyhole and wouldn't tell us how the doctor had made the baby, who later turned out to be Little Pete, whom Jon called Repeat.

Stern as a poker, Grampaw eyed us, saying, "Questions such as them are out and out sinful!"

We had figured Grampaw would know since he and Granny had all those kids.

He sent us skirting round back to the kitchen where somebody fed us buttermilk and cornbread. We suspected we should have been in on what was happening in that bedroom,—the baby belonging to us as much as we both belonged to each other, and more than we belonged to anybody else.

The adults had their own world and it was far away from where we roamed. Our job was to calculate how we could get by and get what we wanted without getting them upset or having them interfere with our adventures.

Naturally, Jon was my hero; and I followed at his heels with complete devotion, like later my fourth year when we were wandering down by the road barefoot and he stepped into a nest of yellow jackets.

The minute it happened and they stirred up into an angry mess, he took off up toward the porch. I ran after him, right through the swarm. He slammed the screen door and latched it so the bees wouldn't get into the house.

Only a few of the crazed varmints had managed to sting him; but when Granny and Mamma came running toward the fit I was pitching, they found me covered with critters bound on revenge–under my dress, in my panties, my hair.

Mamma tore my clothes off while Granny got the lead tub and filled it with buckets of water she and Jon had toted in from the well. After I was dunked several times head to foot, the bees let go. There were lots of them left floating light as baby dandelions while I was doused all over with baking soda.

Except for my pride and a multitude of whelps, I was pronounced lucky not to be allergic to bees and told I would probably never in my old age have aching joints. That didn't mean an awful lot to me then, but I never have had arthritis. Anyway–the whelps sure earned me a lot of attention. Jon sat across the room with his tongue clenched between his teeth, leering at my moment of tragic drama, looking more entertained than sorry.

It must have been later on that summer when Jon cut my foot with the ax, because I don't recall having any bandages on my foot when I got stung by those bees. My only memory is that we were at the woodpile where we were not allowed and Jon was splitting wood. As I grew up, I had always supposed I had edged up too close to his swing–and the blade hit my foot instead of the wood.

A couple of years ago, we were sitting around a picnic table with other cousins who had gathered from far and wide for the annual family reunion. We had just met Odetta and Wilkie's new grandchild; and Jon and I got to talking about how we used to spy on the courting.

Wilkie raised an eyebrow and said, "We knew you were there, every time. Not only were we aware of you watching, but I had to come stocked with Juicy Fruit gum to bribe you away."

We had forgotten that part. I got to talking about my scar, taking off my shoe to show how lucky I was to have not lost a foot for putting it where it was not supposed to be.

"Accident?" Jon said, "I didn't chop your foot by accident!"

He took off his left shoe and sock and propped up a bare foot which sported a cantaloupe scar in the same place as mine. He looked me in the eye and continued with relish.

"You were the one with the ax, trying to chop wood, and you lost your balance on your swing and hit my foot instead."

Jon took a deep breath and looked around at his audience.

Urged on by the chuckles of my cousin, Mary Ellen, Aunt Pauline's daughter from Pittsburgh, he said,

"Man, that stung like the devil and I guess I wanted to get you back–and yeah–an eye for an eye, little sister–!"

I gaped across the table at my grinning hero's big foot, and over his toes to where his tongue clamped between his teeth, and had visions of bees–hundreds, swarming in the thick heat.

4:30 PM

Vedi is back on my continent. The nurse said he called from Kennedy airport with a ticket for the first flight to Charlottesville. I close my eyes and picture him on the plane. Spears of light make a colored spectrum on his window, shattering onto his face like daisies. His eyes are heavy against the lights. He lifts his brow the way he does, straining to hold them back from sleep.

Vedi's eyes have soaked up the Aegean since he left me, combed rich fields of poppies or wheat, row on row swayed in warm winds. He has swept across the coppered hills of Anatolia like a surveyor trying to decide value. I've watched him considering his native soil as if he were going to purchase it. In fact he rather does, buys it up again in his brain, and tucks it away in files. I can detect when he pulls out those files, not very often, but sometimes in those brief moments. Like when I come upon him sitting on the balcony on a Saturday at sundown. His eyes this past month will have tried to absorb all those flavors,–tomatoes about to burst, cucumbers crisp off the vine, mounds of shiny black olives, cheap and common feta cheese. Most of all, I hope he has had enough good conversations in his own language to satisfy him for a while. Coffee with his mother. *Ana*–skin like weak tea, almond eyes tangy-rich. He will have kissed her soft hand, savored its lemon scent. Her hand to his head in respect, in goodbye, he will have been wondering again if this time is the last.

Finally, he'll be in Charlottesville. He'll lean back into the seat of the cab, take in a deep breath like he's trying to inhale all the lush green of Virginia, after being in that part of Turkey where there's wide stretches of brown merely spotted with green. He'll notice how the green touches the sky. Last time we returned together I pointed out that very thing to him.

His cab will pull up to the curb somewhere down below this hospital. He will be only minutes. He'll race up the steps. Like a habit, his going into hospitals, feeling at home. He likes this university because so much of it was designed by Jefferson.

From this bed I can see through the doorway down the hall. I'll see Vedi coming before he sees me.

In his time, he has watched children die from cancer, put his hands inside abdomens gashed open by knives, and cleaned-out a world of abscesses.

What will he think of this?

6:35 PM

Five of the thirty-minute "visiting hour" this afternoon have been scratched away by the clock. Twice, I thought I heard the quickened pad of Vedi's feet. Why is he late?

The nurse is finished with replacing a saline solution bag for the old man on my left. She turns and pauses to look at me, the empty bag in her hand.

"How are you doing, Judy?"

She stretches her shoulders up and back. I take another deep breath and push it out to relieve my tension, which is my way of answering her question.

"Are you sure my husband said he was on his way?"

She chuckles. "Oh, yes he did." Then she looks toward the door.

Like the magic of a genie appearing on request, he is here. My throat constricts as I suck back the flood of emotion that wants to spill out of me. My eyes focus first on his brown leather belt, and I note it has been let out a notch. The khaki suit we bought before he left shows the creases in the groin and elbows where he doubled in the seat to sleep his nine-hour flight across the Atlantic. He's wearing a purple Izod shirt, probably the only one he did not give away to nephews before he left Turkey. My eyes climb under his broad neck and around his chin. A fresh tan exaggerates his jowl, and sets the wrinkles deeper in his cheeks, around his eyes, and makes pockets of his dimples. His whole face is pulled into a soft smile directed at me. His lips pucker in a silent kiss, then he says,

"Hi Baby." His eyes are moist.

The nurse, on cue, walks toward the door. As he steps aside to let her pass, she is lilting, "Judy's been counting the minutes here waiting for you."

I'll have to get a grip on myself, be careful how I speak. He is not a man who cries easily and I couldn't stand for him to do it now. He must not know how frightened I have been. The fear is in the box. I had thought that I would hand it over to him. Yet, right now, I realize I can't do that.

I draw my lips tight and curve them up. "I'm fine, really."

He is at my bed in a second. Our arms reach for each other in the old familiar way. He smells sweet. I am kissing his neck below his ear tasting and breathing in Obsession cologne as his hands are smoothing warmth onto my shoulders and down my arms. The Obsession is a reality check. He is actually here. I feel a tingle move from my abdomen and pulsate at each side of my neck.

"I've missed you," he whispers. I know what he means.

He pulls back, holding both my hands. I shrug, trying to mimic, "Can you believe this?" I want to make light of the situation. If both of us act as if we can bear it alone, we can bear it together. That's always been the rule.

Vedi moves again through the space between us and drops his head to my breast, half hugging the bedclothes. I can feel my heart beating against his ear and imagine stripping away these cords. I am guessing he might have similar thoughts, even in this sterile scene. I run my fingers through his curly hair. It is damp with sweat.

"I'm sorry you have to find me in such a state."

He raises up. Kissing my hand, he tells me, "The important thing is that you are going to be fine."

He grabs a chair and scrapes it across the tile and positions it so he can sit close. We have so much to discuss.

"Tell me what happened to you. I was late because I stopped to talk with your doctor."

"They think I have the Guillain-Barre syndrome. Have you ever heard of it?"

Vedi nods his head and folds his arms in the manner he does when he is into a serious discussion. "I saw patients with it a couple of times, but I never treated it, of course, it's not surgical, but we hope you do have GBS."

He waits for me to respond.

"If I only have a syndrome, I'll be up and out of here in no time."

Vedi raises his half-moon brows. "Just take it easy, could take some time." The way his eyes are widened, I wonder if he knows something I don't.

I brush through how the numbness started and the rush that brought me here. "They are talking about doing a blood plasma transplant, Vedi."

He is stroking the side of my face and studying my cords and monitor as he says all too casually, "It's a procedure, we shall see later."

He stands and bends, sloppily kissing my lips like an old bull dog. "Do I smell like onions? I had a hamburger at Kennedy—I missed that American thing, couldn't refuse the onion."

I laugh. "Who would worry about a little onion in a place like this?"

My nurse comes and starts checking the blood pressure of the young woman on the right. Vedi takes two steps backwards. Maybe it's because of the nurse, but his whole posture turns doctorish.

"OK Judy, you are not to worry," he tells me, using his professional voice. "You got the best neurologist around. I will be checking your chart, talking with the doctors, taking care of everything. Meanwhile, rest."

Rest?

He puckers me another silent kiss, raises his finger to his lips then up to the clock, signaling that visiting time is over.

I pull at his hand. "Come on, you're a doctor. They're not going to run you off so fast!"

He looks around and takes a step toward me.

I begin talking rapidly as if to hold him to me: "Sweetheart, the nurse said the Guillain-Barre syndrome's been around a long time, though I sure never heard of it, said it used to be called The Ascending Paralysis, in the polio family."

Vedi sits again, nodding quietly in agreement.

"I can't understand why it's called a syndrome. I wonder if I'm imagining this paralysis."

He is mouthing, "No."

I lean forward and agree. "No, can't be, Doctor Miller said it's caused by a virus which gets in the body and tricks the immune system. They ask me if I've had a virus recently, but I haven't, not even a cold."

Vedi studies me. "You haven't been sick at all the past month, not even feeling run-down?" he asks.

"Absolutely not. In fact, I've been feeling good."

"It's curious," he says. "You are very lucky."

"Listen, I first thought back in Roanoke that Gene Godwin said I might have the Green Beret."

Vedi scrunches up his face in confusion.

"When he told me what he thought was wrong with me there in our bedroom. Guillain-Barre, Green Beret, get it?"

Vedi grunts.

"They say this virus has tricked my immune system to destroy the peripheral nerve system."

"You've got the idea of what we know about GBS."

"I picture this virus as hundreds of camouflaged beings with blackened faces and helmets creeping through the jungle beneath my skin."

"That's an interesting analogy, yes, cutting communications to your brain, trying to take over everything."

After he kisses me goodbye the last time, I lie listening to the muffle of his shoes being engulfed in the din of noise. Like a thick fog, the din folds over his path down the hall. I am worn-out, as if I have just done an hour of aerobics. The top half of my body feels as if it is wrapped in gauze. But I'm still wide awake.

I am picturing how tomorrow Vedi will take my hand, purple and swollen from needle punctures, and the cords will be disconnected, and I will feel the ache evaporating and I'll start to tingle on the soles on my feet, and feelings will be rapidly coming back to my legs as I stand up—and then we will finally be headed back toward home, where this whole episode will only be a wild story for us to tell at dinner parties.

Last year, in Turkey, Vedi and I drove with Kevin and Karen from Antalya to Alanya past rock beaches, pebble beaches, brown sand, gray sand, calm turquoise waters where creeks and rivers rush to the sea, past Hellenistic castles, Byzantine churches, Selcuk castles, there, we flew high above waters, no guard rails.

Beyond Antalya, the wheat fields were burning, turning the stubs of what was liquid gold blowing in the early summer sun to black, burning off the gold, making ash in the air—the leaping flames mandarin against the molten dusk—the ponderous smoke, the rushing cars. No visions of our past could intrude on that scene, it was so much to take in. The fields were alive with a ghost dance. The air was all hemp, brown crust and ash.

The Gypsies clustered by the creeks, their tents heaped up like unmade beds, their skinny children running, playing tag. Migrant workers, they were there to lay the wheat in bundles, to tie and heave them onto wooden wagons. Horses had toted them to town to be bread and so the rubble and stubs of gold like "crew cuts" were glowing in the dusk and the Gypsies again free with lira to dance and drink in the sunset while our cars cut through the matted smoke that mixed with our exhaust fumes and the wide lands lay blackened for another day.

In and near the towns, the fat, absolutely fearless white, crusty chickens came to the roadside and darted close to the whirling tires. They were skilled in finding what they needed to survive, hardly ever was one of them off in their timing, their legs so quick near the rolling wheels. They dedicated themselves to their task, seemingly oblivious to pedestrians or passengers. The hens brought their brood as soon as they were feathered and the little ones had caught on fast. Inbred from years of the modern rush, those chickens knew not the need to get to the other side.

In Antalya, Kevin, Karen and I walked barefooted on the pebble beach, all round colored stones ground by the tides and pitched back onto the shore, stones fallen from the mountains that leer out over the Mediterranean. The stones hurt our feet but it was too wonderful not to walk there. We chose some to bring home: brown laced with white, blue with black pits, jade green. The whole afternoon wrapped us in a concert of wind and colors. The giants of marble and agate loomed above us. Storms of many seasons had torn at them, continually stealing jagged bits of their hard bone, gradually honing mountain to pebble—in time to sand.

2

Jordan's Stormy Banks

Monday, July 7, 1:00 AM

I can't move my head, not even a quarter of an inch. My thoughts float in a dark and thick lake of pain. They did a spinal tap on me six hours ago to check the protein in the fluid.

"I don't understand," I said. My intuition told me not to let them do it.

"A simple procedure," they said. "Dr. Miller thinks it should be done." And Vedi said to rely on my doctor's judgment.

The neurology resident came with his needle and tubes. They put me in a fetal position. He punctured my spine.

Now, if I move my head in the least, I get volcanic pain. They told me, "Lie absolutely flat and you won't get pain." I have not since raised my head. It even hurts when I blink.

"Give me some Tylenol or aspirin. " I am begging.

The nurse eyes me for a few seconds. "It'll go away soon," she says, "This reaction almost never happens. You must have moved. They told you not to move."

I mouth a "No," for I don't dare shake my head. "Please," I whisper.

The nurse sighs. "Judy, you can't have anything yet. You'll have to grin and bear it for a little while."

She walks away. The phosphorescent lights sting. My strung-out nerves wince at the sound of the scuffing of her steps. Minute fur-balls of energy go running up and down my veins like the coyote in some continuous *Roadrunner* cartoon, howling through the canyon of my head.

Thoughts of dying stalk my mind. During these long hours, feeling strange and useless, suspended in time and space, I analyze isolation. This is the true state of all human beings.

You come in to the world alone and you go out of the world alone.

I've heard my mother say that a hundred times. People can touch me in the space I occupy but no one can quite enter my reality. I feel so alone on an edge of darkness. If I fall over, what will happen? Will anything catch me? I have always said I believed in the afterlife. Do I really? I use everything I know to hold my teetering body here on this edge. My spirit dances around my fixed body.

If I die, life will keep on going. My spot will be taken just like that. My little life of running around doing all those things to justify my existence can be snuffed over like one sweep of a brush across canvas.

The night manager, with a self-assured smile, told the others goodnight at the door of the restaurant. To take a cab those six city blocks at eleven at night would drain the tips Gladys needed to put food in the mouth of her three kids.

Under the lights from the lampposts, the streets were surreal and stark. Gladys pulled her cloth coat around her breast and buttoned it, holding her purse under her arm, its straps over her shoulder. Her white nurse's shoes allowed her ease in taking broad strides. An occasional car flashed its beams on her as it whooshed past. She kept looking to her sides, examining bushes and large containers, then beyond her, where she would cross the street and head for the viaduct under the railroad tracks.

She glanced up. The stars were moth-eaten holes in a dark cloth.

She could not make out any of their patterns except the "Big Dipper." It was too far away to pour any coins of fortune on her head–and anyway, Gladys didn't believe in magic.

The viaduct was full of cars and walkers in the morning; but at night it was a tunnel, looming toward her. Once she got out of it, she would take a left. Then, she only had to go down a block and cross the street in front of the Nabisco plant. The three-story house she was headed for had been built in the century's turn and had since been expanded with stairways added outside. Gladys pictured herself climbing the wooden steps to the one room flat that she shared with her three youngsters and her husband. Jewel was an electric sweeper salesman–when he wasn't drinking. He kept the kids at night while Gladys waited tables at Jim's Spaghetti House, but she knew it was the kids who took care of him on nights when he got loaded. Gladys comforted herself with the thought of how nice it was going to be to crawl under warm covers. She slept with five year-old Judy and two year-old Pete. Jon took the couch, and Jewel had a cot.

The October air was crisp. A few dead leaves rattled across Gladys' path as she entered the underpass. The rhythmic slough from her shoes bounced off the black walls. She wished some cars would happen by so as to light things up. She had been meaning to buy a flashlight.

Halfway through, and Gladys heard heavy squeaks. Clodhoppers or boots. She paused and turned but didn't see anything. She picked up her pace. The noise came faster. There was someone back there.

She began to run, clutching her black vinyl purse to her like a pillow, unable to keep a steady, quiet breath. Whoever was behind her would know she was scared.

The squeak became a steady clop. Gladys tried to watch the breaks in the concrete beneath her feet so that she would not stumble, but it was hard to see. The small lights on the viaduct walls were filthy and not much help.

She ran faster. If something happened to her, would Jewel pull himself together and care for the kids? She knew that he could be a good worker when he wanted to be. He just had this problem that he couldn't seem to work out. Gladys couldn't dare to wonder what the kids were doing in the evenings while she was dishing out spaghetti–with the smile and air of composure that had earned her the position of night manager. Jewel had *never failed to pick up Judy and Pete at day care, but there was no phone at the flat; so she had to work with that uneasy feeling in the back of her mind.*

Gladys was breathing in gulps when she came out of the mouth of the tunnel. Her heavy pockets of change were tingling like a tambourine. Good thing the pockets were deep and that she had evened out the tips into both sides. She threw back her head. The "Big Dipper" appeared smaller.

Gladys dashed across Eighth Avenue, not checking for the fast cars that would flash out of nowhere at night. On the other side, she turned and stared at a man in a jacket and cap running up out of the viaduct, coming straight at her.

She took off down the sidewalk and then across the patches of grass until she came to the base of the wooden steps with the blue railing. She grabbed the handrail and looked back. He was almost to the yard. She could hardly catch her breath. Her throat was so dry and hard she couldn't scream.

Gladys pulled the rail with one hand and hiked her purse over her shoulder with the other while she climbed two stairs at a time. At the top, she began digging into her purse. She found the key and pounded on the door.

No one answered. She could barely see the keyhole but felt it slip into the slot. The man was on the steps as she turned the lock. His feet trounced the steps like big stones.

She slipped inside, pressed a hip against the door and clicked the lock. Pale shadows draped the objects in the darkened room. She glanced around, counting her three precious heads. Jewel was snoring and breathing out the stench of Early Times again. It would be tough luck rousing him.

The man outside shoved hard against her. She put her full weight on the inside of the door, whispering, "Jewel, help me!"

In the dim light through the window, she caught the glint of the butcher knife on the table. She took two steps, grabbed it, and pushed her shoulder into the door while she rammed the blade up to the hilt into a slit halfway up the frame.

The man grunted like a bear. Letting her back fall against the door, she braced her legs, dug her rubber soles into the linoleum and felt his weight resisting hers.

Finally he cursed. "Bitch! Tease me, will you!"

She didn't answer, whispering now to God.

Finally, she felt the door's relief. There was rustling, then heavy shuffling away. Gladys relaxed her legs but kept her position. He could come back. He could watch for her tomorrow night. She would have to find a way to afford a taxi. Jewel would hate what had happened. Of course, he would buy a flashlight.

Gladys clutched her side, surprised to find that the straps of her purse were still over her shoulder. She hugged it to her breasts with both arms and bit her lower lip as the stinging tears began to come in a gush. She was careful to stifle her jagged sounds so that the children would not be startled awake.

The smell of spaghetti sauce, parmesan cheese and Early Times collided as she dropped her purse and began to wipe her face with her hands.

4:00 AM

Linda comes. "I thought you might want this on your head to ease your pain." She is balancing wonderful, wet towels on her palms. I sigh as she lays it across my forehead, adjusts and smoothes my sheets. "I know it's been rough," she says quietly.

I look up at her. "Let me ask your opinion," I say. She nods and leans nearer to me. "The night my paralysis started–I should have called the doctor right away, but I put it off like nothing was happening. How could I have been so stupid?" The high-pitched staccato from the old man's monitor bleeps the seconds away.

"You feel guilty?" she asks.

I look away, studying the ceiling as if there is some formula there between the lines of the cracked plaster.

I drop my eyes back to Linda. "Well, surely I knew something was wrong when I woke in the middle of the night. Do you think it was because I really thought I was going nuts?" The chill of the compress creeps across my scalp.

Linda bends closer. "I hear about that kind of reaction to sudden trauma all the time," she says. I am puzzled.

"Look," she whispers, stretching in toward me again, "Consider that it was paralysis happening to you that night." I wait and she continues. "The five stages of facing terminal illness. Do you know what is the first stage of acceptance of death?"

"Denial," I answer, scooting my head just a bit from left to right. The cold sensation from the compress sinks into my cheek bones. A pain rolls across my forehead.

"Bingo." Linda states matter-of-factly. "You were experiencing a dying in your legs, Judy, and you were denying it with all the reserve you had."

Linda's forthright explanation washes over me. Of course! I take in a long breath and slowly exhale. "And calling the doctor would have been to admit. As long as I denied it, maybe it was not happening." Linda nods her head. "So, I didn't want to be embarrassed by calling a doctor for something which I didn't want to think was really happening." I feel a sense of relief. "My ego, denial, and fear were easier to handle than the guilt of thinking I had neglected proper action."

"Hey, you might just skip the anger step and go right into the bargaining step," she laughs. She turns, and I close my burning eyes against the lights.

Eight year-old Judy hears the lilt: "Blue bells, cockle shells," and the yelling: "Red rover, send Buster right over!" of recess. Each bounce and gravel-scattering thud seems far away. A cider-shaded leaf wafts through the Indian summer air, drifting to where she scrunches her toes in black and white oxfords. The raggedy wind yanks at the paisley cotton shirting her knees.

"Don't ever pick up any chewed-on-gum and put it in your mouth. You'll get a dreaded disease and die a pitiful death from it."

Her mother's voice has jars through her mind just as the bell signals the end of recess. Judy is pondering something stuck on the underside of one of the steps on the fire-escape. She thinks that the iron structure looks like a big preying mantis clinging to a brick wall.

The playground groups begin to gaiter toward the double-doors. The bell clangs for fifteen seconds, but Judy doesn't budge–as if her ears are padded with muffs. Her green eyes are fixed on a wad of bubble-gum on the belly of the mantis. Its sticky-pink color shows it has barely been chewed, maybe just enough to get the easy rhythm going between the teeth and over the tongue; but not enough to milk out the sweet juice.

Her stringy strawberry-blonde hair lifts nervously in the wind and tickles at her cheek. The other kids are swarming over at the door like sweatered bees. If she doesn't hurry, she will be late and Miss Doak will wrinkle up her eyebrows and put her in the brown chair in the back corner again. She'll have to sit there listening to the other second-graders cutting out their black cats and purple witches. The best ones get to be hung from the windows.

Out of the slant of her eye, Judy catches the tail of the last sweater through the door. A decision has to be made. Any kids caught with gum has to carry it up to the front of the classroom on the palm on their hands and plop it in the basket while everybody watches. Then, their name gets put on the blackboard's bad list. But Judy knows how to hide chewing gum under her tongue.

The pink glob on the mantis looks just like a mother cat's tit, almost like it is ready to fall down into her mouth–probably it's Double-Bubble, the best you can buy. In a flash she's reached up, loosed it with one quick twist and stuffed it between her lips. She clamps up and down on it, milking the fruity sweetness as she runs to be the last one through the door.

In the next hour, the class is busy cutting and pasting, each child envisioning his and her witch, cat or pumpkin hoisted onto the brown tassels at the windows. No one notices the little strawberry-blonde criminal working at the middle table. Carefully, she keeps her lips poised together while she moves the mass in and out between her teeth, probing with her tongue but controlling the urge to shove it through the wad and blow.

Walter, whose stuff always gets hung, is working his way around the room distributing scissors from a basket. In too big a hurry, Judy has snipped off her cat's tail; and now, she spreads the white paste, smoothing it out like peanut butter. She carefully lines up the rough edges, then bends closer, rubbing the ends together with a finger. The blunt line still shows.

A drop of pink spit hits the belly of the cat. The splat was a slip. Judy has let her tongue poke through her lips with the gum molded around its end. She quickly raises her eyelids to see Walter staring at her from across the table. It's too late. His possum eyes widen then narrow as his thin mouth curls at the edges. Walter, who would never disobey Miss Doak or his mother, loves to tattle.

He eases out across the room. Judy slips her hand up and over her mouth, dumping the now tasteless lump into her fist. It clings to her palm as she tries to shove it into the black and purple clutter of construction paper. She slides across the aisle and sticks it under the table where the new boy sits. By the time ole Dumpty-Doak and the rest of the class have turned around, Judy is smiling broadly, holding up a cat with crippled tail.

Hours later, Judy rides home in the back of the yellow bus. Out the window, the houses pass in blurry grays. She has managed to escape the chair. But, what of "the greater consequence" that Daddy always emphasizes? One thing she knows for sure: by now the forbidden treat has all melted into her body, been carried from her stomach to her blood,–like the poster on the bulletin board shows, the picture of the naked man with his skin rolled back. "There's no changing what's done," her mother likes to say.

For a long month, she waits for the dreaded disease to strike. The girl they know as Judy will die a horrible death; and she'll be gone forever from the lunchroom, the playground, the hills with beechnut trees. Never again, will anyone see her in the front yard hopping on the teeter-totter Daddy bolted to a stump. Mother will not have to pick up her shoes.

She doesn't mind the horrible death. Or the dying. People will gather round, pitying her and insisting she eat just a little more ice cream, which she will be noble at doing, managing to smile a bit as she shows great courage in trying times. She can handle that. But what nags at her is that when the disease strikes, Mother will KNOW how she disobeyed. Judy dreads that look that she's seen too often. Mother will say, "How COULD you do such a thing after you've been told?" When Jon finds out she's dying, he'll be sorry for all the mean things he's done. Judy can't tell him yet, he'd snitch; but once she gets the disease, there's nothing to worry about. Daddy could never lay the switch to a suffering, mere whisp of a thing, which is about all that would be left of her.

Daily, she watches for the signs,–red marks on the legs, a feverish head or sores on her tongue. But, nothing, not even a boil.

The days drag on into December. One afternoon, like all the others, the yellow bus stops to let off. The door snaps open and the pukey fumes seep in after the engine gives a big belch. Judy studies a penny-sized lace doily that's floated against the window. Any time now, the snowflakes will be covering up everything. She's waited so long, even the cut-outs hanging from the window of the classroom have changed. Her Thanksgiving turkey didn't get hung neither, although Walter not only got his turkey picked, but he got to be Miles Standish. Judy was one of the Indians. Lot she cared, cause she figured she was dying anyway. But she hasn't even gotten a fever. One day, at lunch, she almost felt like she was going to throw up, but didn't.

As the bus rumbles away from the curb, she watches the flake dissolve into a bead that slides down the glass and pauses at her eye-level. The flake doesn't disappear; it merely changes. She stares into the bead as if it were the crystal ball the Gypsy had at the school fair in October. Slowly, it comes to her: ADULTS DON'T ALWAYS KNOW EVERYTHING. The bead breaks off the window and flies away.

Hilarious laughter unravels outside the NICU door, an explosion that happens when listeners finally get the punch line of a long joke. I open my eyes. The jab of a cramp feels like a knife in my back. I wrestle my shoulders against the sheet where it's been lodged too long in one position. My eyes cringe against the overbearing fluorescent. I wonder when are morning visiting hours. I study the hands of the clock.

Get a dreadful disease.
Mother didn't say how long it would take.

7:30 AM

One of the resident doctors is standing at the desk, reading my chart. There must be fifteen of them assigned to follow my case. Hour after hour they come to practice on me, using the same routine. I've memorized the sequence of their questions.

"Now, Judy, giving us the answers before we ask is not cooperating."

"Is it really necessary each of you hear No to the same questions?"

"To which questions are you referring?"

"Did you eat raw fish in the past month?

"How many toes am I moving?

"Did you have minor surgery?

"Which foot am I touching?

"Can you feel the match zip across your sole? Have you had intestinal upset lately?"

They've started moving the order around so that I can't answer before they ask, while they tap on my limbs with little rubber hammers, prick the soles of my feet with needles, and flex my toes and legs. But they give me no medication.

"Have you had a virus or digestive sickness recently?"

"I repeat—flu in February—and the same flu in April. Each bout lasted a month."

"Too long to be a connection. Anything else?"

"Had the same flu in April that I had in February. Is it possible the same virus hid in my system between those months?"

"Not likely."

"Why is there no relationship to this GBS? It's supposedly caused by a virus."

They just shake off my question.

Neurologists mostly seem to be a serious lot, as is this young resident with me now. He is approaching my bed, looking to be lost in thought.

"How are we doing today?" he says dryly.

I take a breath to steady my head. Perhaps I'll try a bit of humor to see if he will react. "Do you know what irony is?" I ask softly.

"Excuse me?" he answers, bending nearer by head.

"Irony," I continue, "is the fact that I arrived in this place not-sick-only-paralyzed, and now you guys have managed to make me not-only-paralyzed-but-sick."

The young doctor looks like he hasn't slept enough for days, and also like he might need some grandmother to take him home and fatten him up a bit. He stands with his arms folded across my chart and regards me without changing his expression. I guess that he is deciding whether to start hammering on my foot or on my knee. Since he doesn't answer, I am stranded in the muck of my stupid comment. I have an urge to scream. My head would shatter like a plate-glass penthouse. I envision my mouth as a beaver's dam.

The resident turns around when the voice of my doctor bounces through the door. The head of the department is making morning rounds with his staff. He bursts into the room, with a hearty, "Good morning!"

The residents follow in his steps, hanging on his every word. My resident greets Dr. Miller, handing him my chart and stepping back to let the Chief come nearer to me. The others encircle my bed. I picture myself: I am their CASE, an object, a puzzle for them to solve.

"Patient has been experiencing severe reaction to the spinal tap since seven last evening. It is being followed, expected to dissipate soon," Miller says. "–SO," he continues, bending to me, "Judy, are we feeling BETTER this morning?"

"Not really, Dr. Miller, can't you give US something for our pain?"

"I'm afraid not yet," he answers. The residents are a bunch of bobbing heads on starched white floating in the space above my body.

I am discussed in the third person mode. "She." "The Patient." I am a cardboard cut-out, a paper doll on which things are stuck.

Diagrams run from my head to toes, a little tag with a blinking light hanging from the sheet where my toes pyramid. Another is pinned onto my left ear, which is with each second blooming red as a carnation. I might just turn into lemon jell and dissolve. Then they will really have a puzzle. "Where did she go?" they'll ask, probing and pounding the pillow. But there will be nothing to analyze but a suspicious sticky smear on the mattress, which, of course, the nurse will find when she changes the bed for the next Patient. The residue of me will test to be slightly tart, perhaps containing just a bit too much acid.

"So." Dr. Miller is expounding. "I'm ordering an MRI test. Her hyperactive reflexes could indicate the need to rule out several areas of concern—therefore, I am led to believe the problem might yet be a myelitis involving the central nervous system."

Reflexes. I suddenly realize I have something they need to know. I raise a hand and begin to wave it slightly as I interrupt him. "Could I say something?" I ask, touching my cheek with my other hand, as if to hold back the waves of pain. "Excuse me down here, I want to tell you something."

Dr. Miller stops abruptly and looks at me. The others immediately assume his stance. They have shifted their focus to my face. I like doctors. They are for the most part truly concerned human beings. Through the years I've had them at my table, joked with them at cocktail parties. Almost always, these dedicated people are willing to listen. They love doing a good job. You just have to get their attention. Now, here are nine of them waiting to hear what I have to say, another doctor's wife trying to give her opinion. And they will listen patiently if I don't take too long about it. I clear my throat.

"Truth is–" I speak as demurely as I think the present situation will permit. "I have always had hyperactive reflexes in the knees and elbows. There is nothing abnormal in that for me."

Not one expression on eight faces changes, though several of them glance side to side.

"You should know that any doctor knocking on my knees better sit back away from my foot." I smile faintly, as I have attempted another light-hearted remark.

They wait, not blinking. An embarrassment starts my blood surging, and I am sorry I spoke because now my skull is threatening to explode again. All the residents' heads turn to Dr. Miller. He reaches down and takes my hand and pats it gently. Then, he smiles a genuine kindness into my eyes.

"Thank you, Judy. This information will be taken into consideration. Perhaps we might tend to weigh the decision for that test."

He looks around to his team. "You see, here's another good point.

Always ask your patient about symptoms which puzzle you. Often they have answers."

In a few minutes, my doctor is finished with me and has already exited the room, followed by his *protégés*, filing one after the other on his tail coat. I hear them parading on down the hall to the next observation and analysis—like a concerned flock of white penguins.

10:00 AM

Will the time never pass? I am tired, so tired and tired with being tired, two nights with no sleep; and now another long day. Mother and Pauline are telling me what they had for breakfast.

Pauline is laughing. "Ate so much I thought I was going to pop."

They don't know what else to talk about and I don't feel like talking much because of my head. They pause, looking quickly at each other, Pauline raising an eyebrow. "Anyhow," Pauline says, "Pete and Vedi are trying to catch up with your doctor to see what he thinks."

Mother's eyes fill with tears.

"Now, don't start again Gladdy," Pauline says, moving closer to her and taking her by the elbow.

"No, I won't," Mother says, swallowing and wiping at her nose. "I just want you to know we are here as long as you need us."

Pauline shakes her head. "And your mother is going to make arrangements to come back to Roanoke so's she can take care of you for a while when you get back home."

We speak briefly about when that might be, but nothing has been said of it to anyone.

When they leave I feel torn. I don't want them to go, but I can't think of what to say to them while they are with me. I'm weary of trying to fight. Vedi has told me the doctors are thinking positive because the paralysis hasn't progressed further. They are watching now to see if it will "peak." That's what they say when the paralysis shows a sign of regression.

1:00 PM

I am taking some fantastic mind-journeys, like I've never had before except in sleep. Maybe it's out of the body experiences. When I close my eyes it's as if my eyeballs sink like pebbles into a pool at the back of my head. That's followed by a sound of dry wheat scattered across wood. I see a summer wind pick up the wheat and swirl it until I, too, am caught up, lifted free with winds that begin to stretch through colors and shapes on the earth and in the sky: Dancing with daisies in English gardens, viewing Red Square from atop a tree, stringing like a green silk scarf on tombstones, Greek walls, abandoned temples, skimming among fresh mint and just-ground curry in a Bangkok marketplace, veering around silver-edged glaciers dripping in the heat of a gold sun, or adrift in caves of the ocean floor. Bubbling pinks, greens, and reds splash and drift.

I am ebbing in such a sea of rainbows when something pulls me sharply back to phosphorescent light.

Reluctantly, I raise my lids, squinting against the brightness. It stings like pins. I tell myself to relax and concentrate on feeling the support of the mattress.

In my right leg—something is happening, a sensation like a jerk and twitter. My mind rushes to full attention, reinforced by a rapid dose of adrenaline. I hold my breath.

Did I feel movement in my leg?

Or have I only imagined it? I silently exhale. My heart's beating bongos on my temples. The air is stuffy. Moisture seems to be evaporating from the walls.

Then, again, it comes! Like a small, thin thread unraveling at a point in my thigh just above my knee. I gather my energy into my solar plexus and flush it toward that point.

Ever so slowly, as if in reflex only, my knee, of its own will, is pushing the sheet up into a tent several inches high.

I swallow fistfuls of the stuffiness around me and hold it, checking on either side of me to be sure I am not still daydreaming. My two companions are in their beds, their machines beeping, their bodies wheezing in their normal way.

Now I am breathing in heaves, attempting to pull my head and shoulders forward, my eyes riveted on my knee.

There's the familiar rustling, and from the corner of my eye I see the white of Nurse Sally as she comes. Her voice has a high-pitched edge to it. "Are you all right, Dear?"

I don't dare turn my head for fear I might lose this mirage. My hands are waving and pointing to the bulge in the sheet. "Look! Do you see it? My leg!"

"I do indeed." She is almost squealing, carefully folding back the sheet to uncover my legs.

The right leg is—in reality—bent, and it has pulled up on its own. It is not my imagination.

Sally takes my left hand and squeezes it repeatedly, as if she is gently pumping life into me. "Now let's see what's going on," she says, reaching with her other hand to touch my left leg. "See if you can do it again," she commands, her fingers pushing the right knee back down.

I can't feel her fingers, but, as if in response to the command, or more like as if in magical display, I slide the sole of my left foot several inches up the mattress. It happens so quickly, and I am sure I am not the one controlling it. The right foot again does the same that the left has just done. And here I am—with an unbelievable two knees bent in the full-view of a sane and professional witness.

The nurse claps her hands. "Yea! This is great," she cries.

"Oh my God!" I am shouting. "They moved! Both legs. I'm going to be well!"

"Could be," she says, "I've heard of it happening."

"Oh yes," I say, choking, "Tomorrow, I'll be walking out to the car. I HAVE been dreaming!"

I raise both fists in triumph and she catches them, as we sway back and forth in celebration. Tears ooze from my eyes. Spoonfuls trickle down my cheeks. Sally gives me a bear hug and steps back.

"OK," she says, grasping my shoulders, "Let's see if we can sit up. We're just going to dangle those legs over the side of the bed."

I strain. She heaves. My hips won't be budged. For a good five minutes we both desperately attempt to get some part of my lower self to take any initiative to move on its own again but it is of no use. Both of my legs are still dead as sausages.

Now, in streaming tears, I plead with her. "Help me. Do something. It's got to come. I did bend my knees."

She lays me back on my pillow and smoothes the matted hair back off my face. "Judy, now, just take it easy. I'll page the doctor. You're going to be fine."

She backs slowly away from the bed, trying to reassure me with facial gestures. Then, she slips out of the room.

Calling through the doorway, I scream, "This WAS something, more than the NOTHING I've had for two days–something's more than nothing!"

I turn my head to my inert companion on my right and squall, "And why do you continue to just lie there doing NOTHING all the time! Either get up or go ahead and just let yourself die!"

Even before the two round the bend on Tom's Creek Road where they see the Wayne County, West Virginia Church of God pulsating in the darkness on the top of the knoll, they can hear that the service has already started. Judy knows her cousin's going to blame her with their being late. As they climb the snaky driveway, she scuffs her tennis shoe in the gravel and wiggles her big toe through the frayed hole. Patty's still trudging on ahead, moving toward the open doors. The foggy spray of light from the white wooden building is speckled with indistinguishable fluttering wings and sparkling music. It spills out into the night and onto the grass and steps like a fairy queen's magic spell. The August air feels cool as the rocks at the cistern, and is loaded with the syrupy smells of Queen Anne's lace and primroses. It makes Judy, a Huntington-girl, want to doddle; but Patty motions to her from the steps. It was Patty, fooling with her hair, that made them late; but, no lousy fifth-grader can argue with a fourteen-year-old. Judy trips on her own shoelace as she goes sprinting into the light.

She follows Patty through the doorway where ushers point to a space at the aisle. Everybody's singing, "Shall We Gather At The River?"

Judy takes a minute to get the hang of the tune, then joins in. Patty stiffens. "Do you HAVE to sing tenor?" she whispers. Judy stops, wrinkling up her mouth.

"It's O.K. to sing," Patty continues, "but it's better to blend in, not have people staring."

By the time Judy finds her place again, they're on the third verse. This IS Patty's church, and she did tell Judy not to harmonize, after last night. But, there's others that do, and Judy can't understand why she can't, just because she's a visitor.

Across the aisle, Patty's neighbor, Howard, lumps along the melody a note tardy, belly humping out where two buttons have popped. His familiar duckbilled cap is hooked over the rim of a communion glass attached to the back of the pew in front of him. Billy, Howard's kid, hangs off Howard's shoulder, absently picking the peeling skin off his sunburnt nose, bumping against Howard, keeping the beat as the congregation starts to swell:

"Soon we'll reach the shinin ree-ver, the buu-tiful, the beuu-tiful-al ree—ee-ver . . ."

Moths, gathered at two skillet-shaped lamps at the ceiling, create a shifting puzzle of shadows on the singers below.

The bald man in the black suit at the foot of the altar balances the hymnal in his left hand while the right dips and leaps, trying to yank the crowd into step with the accompanist, whose ring-decked hands relentlessly thrash the piano, insisting it sound full as a five-piece band at a hoe-down. The little church vibrates like heat lighting out over the ocean at night.

At length, with the grand sweeping phrase of, ". . . that flows by the throne of God," the tune is brought to a clattering finish, whereupon the song leader sweeps an arm high and holds it as if he's caught a fly ball, while the accompanist clusters an arpeggio like sleigh bells. Judy's mesmerized, like the rest of the congregation, still hoisting hymnals as if they were gold and gilded. Outside in the bushes, the night bugs continue to fiddle and grind.

Up behind the pulpit, a pool's filled and ready for tomorrow night. "There," the preacher says, "all the newly sainted, with their crowns and hopes of glory, will come, one by one, to be dunked."

The Jordan River flows into the pool from the back wall. The Jordan's a pasty blue with absolutely smooth tan banks, pouring from a green mount, rising from the arid, holy land. Three crosses jut out of a hill, the middle one ringed with a thorny crown.

Everybody sits. Judy pulls a paddle fan from the rack in front of her. HODGES FUNERAL HOME is stamped right into the pile of bread where Jesus has His hands open for the blessing.

"Oh, that was fine, so fine," the song leader is crooning, "It give my heart such comfort to hear you all raise your voice to glory together. I say, REvive us! I say—" The crowd jumps in, with, "ReVIVE us again!"

The preacher has sat down behind the pulpit up on the throne. He's been brought down from Wheeling for this week. He's shouting, "Amen brother, and souls are there tonight waiting for God's hand to carry them on down to HIS river! Yes, Lord, praise God."

Judy sits reverently, very attentive to the presence of her cousin next to her. She wishes she could get Patty to have a little more respect and regard for her. She wonders just what it is going to take. Patty is not really all this big on church, and she makes it clear she's not ready to be saved. Last evening she told Judy that getting up in front of all these neighbors in a white robe and getting dipped would take more religion than she can spare.

And, thinking of religion, Judy's wondering what the Lord thought of her and Patty's smoking corn silks all morning. She liked getting asked, being accepted as old enough to handle a little sin every now and then. Patty had taken her down around the old dirt road to visit some kids whose mother was working. They showed Judy how to roll them up in strips of newspaper. At first, it tasted like rusted iron pipes, but after a bit, she got the hang of it without hardly coughing.

Night before last, out in the meadow, they caught two jars of lightning bugs and brought them back to their room, where the bugs blinked in the dark like spirits, while they made up ghost stories.

Deep down, Patty must really like her. Tomorrow, Judy can go with Patty and her friends to help Howard pick his beans. Afterwards, he'll haul all the gang in the back of the truck to the creek.

This morning when they were smoking together, Patty had said, "By the time we get to the creek, you'll be itching to high heaven to jump in the water, cause nothin's worse than fuzz and sweat from inching in the hot sun down between bean rows; and after a while, you don't know where to scratch because you're itchy all over."

The voice from the foot of the throne gives Judy a start. *"Would anyone have a song THEY would like to sing?"*

Judy has an idea. She darts up her hand and waves it. A surprise for Patty. When he nods to her, she stands.

"I have one I would like to sing." Judy can feel her heart beating in her ears. From the corner of her eye she sees Patty's profile outlined against the fat lady whose dress has creeped up over her spreading thighs, somewhat desensitized by the sleeping baby draped across them.

"What would you like to sing?" the song leader says.

Judy knows. She'll announce it down front. It's appropriate, too, especially since they are pushing the baptism tomorrow night.

She slides out of the pew. The teachers at school tell her she sure has a lovely little voice. Using it for the Lord ought to be the way to go. She needs to work off a little sinning she's done today, too.

She walks the thin maroon-carpet to the foot of the throne where the song leader pats her on the head, saying, *"That number again?"*

"I'm going to sing, `Jordan's Stormy Banks." She speaks right into his widening eyes. *"And, I'd like to dedicate it to my cousin, Patricia."*

He shrugs and gently turns her around by the shoulders. His hands are warm. His voice splashes over the top of her head: *"Friends, it would appear that the Lord has sent us a songbird."*

Judy looks out over the sea of pews, but all she can see is the top of Patty's head.

Judy tells him she doesn't need the piano, so he says, *"Take off!"* and she does. Her feet are firm, toe moving up and down, legs stretched out in a V, like the real performers do it on the Grand Ole Oprey, head thrown back and eyes closed on the most meaningful parts. She's hoping a deeply religious look covers her face, as the faithful attend while she sings, mindful to put the stab on the important words:

"Ooo-on JO-dan's storrmmy banks I STAND-dand cast a wistful eye . . ."

Now, she is really into it, jiggling her shoulders. *"Ohhh, WHO will come and go WITH me, I am bound for the promised land."*

Judy's imagining her bare feet, placed in sun-baked clay at the edge of *a pure, blue-silver river that is stormy and deep. She's not afraid to wade into it, ready to take that step of faith, like the preacher says. She hopes she is making them ALL feel it.*

". . . Sweet Jesus, I am bound . . ."

At the end, they don't even move for a few seconds. Then, they turn to one another and nod.

Yep, it went over good, Judy thinks, figuring how they probably would like to clap, except they are in church.

She feels like she is walking on water, just like Peter, as her legs carry her back to her seat.

She grabs the corner of the pew and swings in. Her skirt makes a "poof!" when she lands. She giggles and looks over to get Patty's reaction.

Patty is scrunched down in the seat on her backbone, arms folded tight across her chest. Judy scoots toward her. "Patty?"

The older cousin doesn't act even a LITTLE bit honored, let alone proud. Her lips are pressed tightly together. She lowers her head and growls. "Move."

Judy's throat lumps. She swallows and begins, but when she speaks, her voice comes in an embarrassing rasp."They ASKED what I wanted to sing."

After a moment, Patty hisses. "Page number. He wanted a PAGE number. Didn't ask you to SING. Last thing I'm doing with you, ever."

In the next hour, the critters outside fiddle and grind louder than ever. Judy wishes she was in the bushes in the dark. She doesn't stir all through the sermon.

And when they call for the invitation, where she had envisioned taking that big step, getting saved so she can wear the robe and be dunked tomorrow night, she is not able to move even one foot—not for all the world and its gold.

3

Green Room

Tuesday, July 8, 2:00 PM

It's as if I'm floating in a frog-green pond, the ceiling, walls, carpet, and blanket of this private room are green as spring. Could this be an omen of rebirth? Through the window across the room there is a lawn and trees.

It's so quiet, no IV's, chords, monitors, undead roommates,—only the spray of rain against the glass. Instead of a clock beyond my toes there hangs a large calendar with a print of one of Monet's paintings of lilies in water.

After having been so carefully watched for over three days, I am suddenly on my own. How will they know if the paralysis starts to creep into my chest? My call button is over there on the tray by the door.

The pill they gave me hasn't suppressed the headache. Since this morning my hands have taken to trembling. When that resident wanted to do another spinal tap this morning, I said, "No."

3:00 PM

"How's my lady this afternoon!" Vedi is calling through the door. His upbeat tone appears a bit exaggerated, but the green room glows with his presence. He walks toward me, placing a paper bag on the portable table.

My right hand goes up into the hair at the back of his head as he bends. His kiss is a reassurance. My world is still functioning.

He studies my bloodshot eyes. "The doctor might give you something to sleep tonight," he says, turning. "Look what I brought you."

From the bag he takes out a spiral notebook, a pen, two sharpened pencils, and a flowered lap pad and lays it on my chest and stomach.

"It's for you to write," he tells me, picking up the call-button-bed-control gadget. My head begins to surge as the bed is raised.

"Don't!" I wail. Fresh jolts of pain start in my head.

He stops it and quickly lowers the bed, a look of hurt on his face. He mumbles. "I always do the wrong thing for you."

"It's all right," I say, forcing a tight-lip smile. I'm so glad to have him here and I want him to know it. He must have jet lag, and it's difficult to wait around a hospital. Again I reach to him.

"I love these things," I tell him, noting that he sees my trembling. "Vedi, come sit."

He gathers the presents, lays them on the table, and drags over the chair. Like adolescents, we rather awkwardly hold hands.

After a moment I ask, "Have you talked with the kids today?" I am relishing the intimacy.

Vedi smoothes his surgeon's palm over my knuckles. "Karen is still staying with Missy. She sends love." He smiles. "She will call you tonight."

My throat aches as I remember Karen's face when I left her.

Vedi clears his throat. "Are you OK?" I indicate yes. "There is more," he says, "Kent and Kevin rang my office this morning. They will be in Roanoke tomorrow."

I am relieved. They are safe. My life is more normal by the minute. "Will they join us here?" I ask.

"Since Kent's going to be here all summer on his job, you'll see lots of him."

"What about Kevin?"

"I'm going to have him stay at home with Karen until your mother gets there."

Vedi crosses his arms. I question with a nod. He raises his left brow. So? What else?" I probe.

For a few seconds he regards me as if considering his words. "Doctor Miller thinks you are stable now," he says.

"But?"

Vedi shakes his head.

"You've most likely got Guillain-Barre syndrome but Miller wants to rule out MS. I also talked with Gene."

"Multiple Sclerosis?"

"Yes," Vedi answers with a little cough. "Gene has only seen one other case of GBS in his practice."

I recall how quickly Gene made the diagnosis on the morning of July 5th. Why do they mention MS?

"Vedi," I ask, "Just what IS Guillain-Barre syndrome?"

"Not surgical," he states. "Named after the Frenchmen who discovered it–an acute idiopathic polyneuropathy which sometimes follows infective illness, inoculations, or surgical procedures." He clears his throat. "But often it occurs in a previously well person like you."

I figure from the way Vedi's rattled it off he's been in the textbooks.

"Yeah," I say, screwing my face to tell him I still don't know what it means.

"Don't worry about it," he says, standing and looking anxiously at his watch. "It affects the peripheral nerves. You've got lots of time to learn all about it–"

Vedi pauses. I can see there's something else he is keeping. MS? Vedi changes his stance, as if he is feeling the weight of my gaze.

"Sit down," I say, "This is a private room."

He is antsy but he sits.

His face brightens. "While I was in Turkey, I wrote all month in the journal you gave me. I decided to view this trip as my odyssey."

"I want to read it."

He nods. "I imagined being both Homer and Odysseus." He grins, looking into my eyes. "In search of a Troy, both still in love with this Helen."

We study one another's face, searching for clues behind our words.

"How did you feel about being there?"

"Like a foreigner," he answers, "Strange, but even my sisters make fun of my accent. I don't even know the new slang. I'm a time capsule."

I look at him—one foot in Turkey and one in America, never could quite be the good ole boy in this country, and he is now an alien in his homeland.

Vedi describes sitting in the sun on a precipice above the Aegean Sea. He was thinking how that spot could be where Homer sat looking out over turquoise, dreaming up a book, and making wars on paper.

"I sat on the cliffs and thought about history, " he relates dreamily. "They say there is a Troy, buried many layers down."

I picture those plains reaching toward the sea. We were there five years ago. The Turks had constructed a huge wooden horse at the entrance to the digs so the tourists could take pictures of their children climbing on its hoofs. We ambled there, musing about the hundreds of ordinary lives gone to the dirt below us, and how those lives could each have been a personal epic. Lives unwritten, lost to posterity. The wind had whipped at my hair and seemed to sigh through the spindly stems of the white asters.

Vedi stands again, adjusting his shirt at his belt, a sure sign that he is absolutely going. Maybe he needs to take a nap. He yawns and breathes deeply before speaking. "Sweetheart, I have to get back home."

My face goes flush. "First you tell me nobody in the medical profession can decide what is wrong with me, and then you tell me you are leaving?"

"You are getting the best care," he continues, "There is nothing I can do here."

My mouth has opened and my jaw tremors a little. I focus on a pimple on his cheek while hearing him tell me he'll, ". . . return to Charlottesville in a couple of days."

I can't believe it. I'm batting angry tears. He takes a step away from me. All those hours of anticipating his arrival. Now he can't wait to wear his mask. My mouth closes. I swallow hard.

"You're going home? How?"

"I rented a car," he says quietly.

He steps forward and pushes my curls from my forehead. "Judy, my office is overloaded. I've been away from my patients for a month."

I don't answer. He begins speaking faster. "I'd stay if I were needed, but you are always strong. Be patient."

I can see he is already gone, out the door, to his profession: his first marriage.

The bubble of intimacy has popped. What's new? He has been running out my doors toward invisible traumas for over twenty years.

One time I even entertained at home eight strangers through an entire evening of dinner: residents and wives whom I thought he would introduce. But he was tied up with an automobile accident case and did not get back until midnight. I waltzed through the whole evening devising ways to address my guests without using their names, which I kept forgetting.

Doctors go to duty like addicts go to dope. That's why most of them marry self-sufficient women. But at this point I can't stride. Three years ago I had a nervous spell that lasted a month. I pulled myself back together. Put it behind me. Got back on my feet. Usually when I am scared I just move faster. How do I make these nerves work again?

"But I'm still in here," I say quietly, as if its an offering.

"Judy, I'm already several days late. Dena's had to shift patients around. I've got surgery I can't put off."

Who am I to compete with sick people? My jaw tightens.

"Oh," he says, fishing in his jacket, "This is for you."

He is dangling a gold chain bracelet in front of my face. "I bought it in Turkey for my bride." His eyes sparkle. "Will you wear it knowing I am with you every minute?"

He is now in his soft and sweet mode. If I said what I am feeling . . .

But, I don't. I made it through the first three nights of this ordeal alone, and by God if I can't now!

I hold out my trembling hand and he hooks the chain around my wrist. My arm falls back to the bed.

As he is going, I ask him to leave the door ajar. Huskily, I add, "Watch out for Calypso."

He laughs, and I know he doesn't have a clue.

I've been scared lots of times. I handle it. Not always well. Mistakes can happen when one is scared. I remember another room. Gray, like a box. Years ago in Pittsburgh. I didn't win any awards for the performance there. Vedi and I had been married only four months. We had come to an appointment at immigration headquarters to deal with his visa. That strange official. He smelled like gym shorts.

Of course, I was scared. I was 22 years old and hadn't yet been introduced to the idea that Girls are children, that Women have choice, or that Sacrifice is not the only virtue that females of honor embrace. I assumed Vedi would be my rock, my comfort and security—although I was tenacious about my *West-by-God* Appalachian independence. Little did I know I was hoping he would be a dependable father. Little did I know that we all have to fill our own needs. I would have to learn how to do that for myself, to be whole.

Quite a shock for us to suddenly get that letter saying Vedi would have to leave the country because we wanted to change his visa status. Seems the quota for the Middle East was low.

At immigration headquarters they separated us. Right away I got the feeling that they were suspicious, as if we were trying to commit some sort of crime. I was the first person in my family ever to be questioned by government authorities. There was no rock to lean on in that room.

They led me to a folding chair in the middle of the room. There was a lady stenographer. The official paced back and forth rattling off questions in a clipped, nasal tone. With his bent knees and forward-thrusted shoulders, he bounced on each step like Howdy Doody, cradling the palm of one hand in the elbow of the other. Sucking on cigarettes while he questioned, he looked to me to be someone trying to imitate a character he might have seen in a spy movie.

"Answer only yes or no!" He shouted at me with that hacking voice. I had always been the perfect, flag-loving United States citizen. Why would they treat me this way?

"Do you know that perjury means prison?"

Prison? I had never even before been to Pittsburgh.

"Did anyone ever tell you that you should marry Ayyildiz? That if you did, he would become a citizen?"

Those words were alarming. Immediately I remembered an encounter the previous summer with one of the other foreign resident doctors when Vedi and I were dating.

"You like the Turk?" the Greek doctor had said.

I said I did.

"Then, why don't the two of you get married?"

I told him Vedi and I hadn't discussed it.

We hadn't.

Did this official think we were guilty?! Had immigration been prying into our personal life in Huntington? Had they interrogated the Greek resident? Could casual remarks be used against us even if they were said to me in jest?

"Marry him. Make him a citizen."

The Greek didn't influence our marriage one way or the other—but a simple yes or no wouldn't be an explanation to that conversation now. I had heard Greeks and Turks were bad karma.

"Well," Howdy was crowing. "Yes or no?"

I couldn't go to jail. I hadn't graduated from college yet!

"No,—I mean, well, yes," I stated. Having his answer, he cut me off.

The next thing I knew, he was asking me if I were pregnant.

I glanced helplessly over to the stenographer.

She looked back with pity although she didn't say a word.

I had missed a period, but it was too early to know for certain. Either answer could be perjury!

"Yes AND no," I said, sniffling. Howdy just dangled a moment, his ashes toppling to the hardwood floor.

After the interrogation the long hassle to get Vedi's visa began, lengthened because of my fearful answer. The visa was delayed three years. But the little YES of the second question was Kent.

After that something had changed. Vedi was still Vedi; but the humiliation in that gray room had removed him from Sir Galahad's horse. To tell the truth, part of me was confused and resentful that I had to defend my loyalty to my country. That strange little puppet of a man in that room in Pittsburgh managed to sow a seed within me that I knew in my mind was not true. But one that nagged at me.

And I resented Vedi for reminding me of my blundering reply to the man's question. For years, Vedi and I found ourselves periodically like wounded soldiers trying to press forward on the marriage field.

6:00 PM

Through the open door I hear wheels, scuffling, and laughter. I smell dinner. I'm hungry, although I really have to be creative to eat with my head down.

I've scribbled a first journal entry in the notebook. My writing is so shaky I'll have a hard time to decipher it.

I may be flat on my back, paralyzed, and God knows what–but, if I die in this frog green room it for damn-sure won't be from grieving over someone's absence. I will leave a few last scrawlings behind. I can still do that for myself.

Footsteps. I turn my head carefully not to rouse the pain. Two orderlies stand in the doorway.

"Ms. Judy, we are here to take you up for testing," the shorter one shouts–as if also I can't hear.

"It's dinner time," I answer.

In seconds they have whisked a litter into the room and positioned it beside my bed.

"It's dinner," I repeat, "I haven't eaten."

"This won't take long, the taller one answers musically. They have to work in these tests as they can, lots of people on the agenda."

I am being careened through a mass of long hallways that connect one building to the other as I look out the Williamsburg panes of the tall old windows, hoping to catch small glimpses of life beyond these walls, and feeling like baggage. I am carted onto an elevator, where I rise several flights; and all this while, the orderlies have been talking about some baseball game. They heave me off the elevator, down a hall, and up to a door.

"Now, don't go anywhere," the tall guy says, throwing me a wink.. "They will come out in a few seconds," he calls over his shoulder as they rush away .

Gloom. There are no windows. But even if they had left me at the gates of Purgatory, I'd have to wait. Long moments stretch to the ceiling and down the hallway. There's no one nearby. Muffled sounds thunder and echo from somewhere far off. I pull the sheet up to my neck. No one. Little doubt my feet are exposed but I can't see or feel them. I hope the orderlies didn't make a mistake. What if everyone has gone home? It's long after five. I could be lost in this vast hospital until morning, stashed in the dusk of this forgotten wing. My body is shaking the cold sheet.

When the door squawks open, a white shadow moves across my side and hovers at my feet. The shadow has a lab coat. I smile the best I have to give, so relieved to have a live person who looks like he knows where he is.

"I am Dr. Daniel, are you Judy Ayyildiz?" he asks.

The space inside looks too small for the cluttered tables and machines. All have cords and knobs. The doctor doesn't speak while he plugs in and hooks up the apparatus. He wheels me over to the machine with the most cords. I think of old movies. *Marx Brothers.*

"We will be testing the responses of your nerves," he states.

I crane my neck to see if he has an assistant. He doesn't.

"This will be a little cold as we fit each end to your head and chest, but we will not hurt."

So, the machine is his assistant. Or maybe the machine is a computer doctor and he is the assistant. It looks as though he is putting Elmer's glue on the button end of each cord.

He begins sticking the buttons to my scalp. When he pulls my hair, I flinch.

"Oh—now don't worry. We won't do any permanent damage."

8:30 PM

I am grateful to see frog green again. I check the wall to make sure the calendar is still here, locate today's number in the square—8. The first test up there wasn't bad; then he began another. Needles, attached to the ends of electrical cords, were stuck deep into my muscles. No wonder he doesn't want to think he works alone. It was the worst thing I've been through, labor and delivery three times included. My head was pounding, my body, clammy. He turned a knob. Electricity surged through the needles.

"This is our low dosage," he kept saying. Tears were running into my ears. "Oh please don't do that," I said.

"We have to measure the nerve damage," he repeated flatly.

I am shaking. Is it coming from the trip to that torture chamber, the cold, or hunger? Let's see: All three.

Short gray hair under a white cap pushes through the door, comes to my bed, and starts taking my blood pressure.

"I didn't get to have dinner."

"Dinner? Dinner's long gone now, Honey," she says, sticking a thermometer into my mouth.

When she's reading it, I say, "I have to get something to eat."

"Honey, you couldn't get a tray now," she laughs, "You should have told them to hold dinner for you."

"Told? Precisely whom?" I say between my teeth, "There was no one watching to tell." I shout, "I'm gonna start screaming rape if you people don't feed me!"

She stands back, appalled.

"I'm hypoglycemic," I say, with a bit more control.

Finally, she returns with six saltines and two slices of processed cheese. And there is a carton of milk and a small plastic cup of lime jello. It seems that in the whole University of Virginia Medical Center this is the only nourishment to be had at nine o'clock at night. Maybe I did die up in the NICU. But I'm sure they will charge my insurance for a full dinner tonight.

Maybe I've been in Purgatory all along. I am so tired. This damned anger is sapping what little strength I have left anyway.

Denial. Now, anger. Second stage.

For the first time in over three days, I fall into a sleep.

I am back up in the NICU and I have fallen out of bed and landed beside the stroke victim. He gurgles steadily on. His wife, knitting a shawl, is sitting in the metal chair beside him.

I find that I am head down, wedged between his bed and her chair, legs stuck straight up in the air, thighs exposed. My thin cotton shift has fallen in rings around my waist.

The wife continues knitting as if there is nothing unusual. I wiggle, finally uprighting myself.

Then, easy as pie, I begin walking through the hospital's maze. Not long thereafter, a man blocks my way. He delivers a telepathic message: THERE ARE NO DOORS OUT OF HERE, and evaporates.

I continue to drift aimlessly and encounter Pete, Mother, and Aunt Pauline. They are carrying huge wrapped presents, a folding table, and a giant panda.

I try to explain, "But there is no room up here for all these things."

I lie in my darkened room and think how I'll be going home in several days, perhaps recovered. They are going to do an MRI tomorrow. I'll get rolled back in a tomb-shaped machine; and maybe when I come out, I will resurrect.

But what if they do discover I have multiple sclerosis?

Just answer yes or no.

Vedi is probably asleep in our bedroom. I try to remember song lyrics and mix the words to "Lay Your Head On My Pillow" with "Send Me the Pillow That You Dream On."

Just forget about tomorrow and hold your warm and tender body next to mine for the good times.

Vedi will turn in his sleep, dreaming of some dancing Helen, my scent on the pillow. My cat will come, lonesome for our nose to nose baby-talk, and so she will be reduced to licking Vedi's toe.

"Come on Kitty," he will mutter, scooping her into his neck.

The two of them will be a warm ball, even though Vedi doesn't care for Kitty any more than Kitty cares for him.

4

Like A Promise

Wednesday, July 9, 6:45 AM

Her voice echoes in my ears, "Get home, now girl . . ."Feet jumping, feet smacking, I'm a hopping frog who knows every inch of this muddy path around the hill, past the outhouse where it zigzags like a snake through weeds up to my shoulders.

Scoot and slide down slippery red clay to a creek that belongs to a snapping turtle. Look down, delight in the way the shadows and lights through the water change the size and forms of my feet so that they skate and crinkle beneath me–ankles are blue in water. Little brown fish with green button eyes and fairy-wing tails kiss my toes.

"Juuu-dee, Ju-dee?"

My billowing dress, a pirate's sail, glides me into a honeyed pasture. Trying to whistle like big brother, Jon, I pucker my lips, blow up against the elephant cloud, cling to the fence. My sandals stirrup in shiny slings, my hands tighten around spikes on the top of the wire. The goldenrod's fuzzy stem tickles my thigh. I become a squishy, red worm on a silver leaf, riding way high, so many legs, I cannot fall.

"Juu-dee!"

Mamma's voice, I have to obey, but I am trying to spot Ole Red. He lopes to the fence. Ole Red can gore, like sticking a pig.

One time, Ole Red got out of the pasture and was heading right towards Granny, who was weeding the sweet peas and cornflowers at the head of her garden. Grampaw jumped up from his rest in the rocker on the back porch and bounded out over the steps and met Ole Red just as he was starting to tromp through the tomatoes.

Grampaw hit that bull right between the eyes and knocked him for a loop, threw a lasso round his neck and led him back through the gate.

My feet slap the path, my mouth waters. I want to spit but I can't stop. The voice pulls my legs. I remember old men at the general store, how they sit and spit brown dandelion splats, chewing like grasshoppers, studying a road of horse-pile wads. My feet make sprats, running toward home.

The voice shatters through a whir of cicadas.

"LAA-DEE, WAKE UP!"

PLACE clangs and bumps. I force burning eyelids.

"WELL, THERE YOU ARE, AND GOOD MORNING!"

The light stings. A woman in blue stands in the doorway presenting a tray.

I glance over to where the pale sunshine wedges through the center folds of the flowered draperies at the window, and before I can turn back to the doorway, a hollow clack follows the whap and click of the door's shutting on the words, ". . . leave you to your breakfast."

The covered tray is sitting on the bed-table, which is next to the chair, half a yard away. Pushing on both elbows, I attempt to elevate my shoulders. The onslaught of trembling lava in my head drops me back to the pillow. I must have fallen asleep sometime toward morning.

A new day. Will my legs move? Try raising the knees. I tighten my diaphragm and pull.

Nothing. Not even a fraction. It's gotten worse! Try again. Gritting my teeth, squeezing my hands into fists against my thighs, I strain. My knees are waterlogged in the sheets. An ache floats from my stomach and catches in my throat. Don't give into it.

I look longingly at the tray.

"Hello–," I shout.

There is no answer. The damn call button is still on the table.

Surely someone will come soon. The doctors. Rounds. They're probably bored with tapping on me.

"Help!" I yell.

This could be embarrassing. What if they hear and come running? I'm not having so much as a heart flutter.

But my blood sure is boiling.

Vedi will be making rounds, tending to his patients three hours southwest.

Your husband's got the best bedside manner.

Patients pull me aside to tell me that.

Over an hour later, the doorknob is turning.

There's a thumb, a hand, a white sleeve, talking: "Pardon my minor nervous breakdown, but it just so happens I'm the only durn one on this floor to do the work of six or eight! RN's pulling charts. Don't even have a Practical this morning. Can't do everything–"

The voice belongs to a buxom blue-haired nurse's aid. "Morning there!" She is chirping.

I begin to answer, "God, I'm glad you're here–"

But before I finish, she states, "Guys here to take you for tests. You're scheduled for seven, and it's now five-of."

She steps aside. The back of an orderly comes through the opening. A litter follows. A second orderly holds onto the end. They swing around parallel.

"No way!" I say emphatically.

I raise, disregarding pain. "Not again on an empty stomach! They put in cold water, then lay me freezing on a table while they stick me with needles they put electric power through!"

The aid wedges hands on hips and tightens her chin like she's thinking: This job isn't dull.

"What do you mean?" she asks.

AM

"Dinner last night, before testing." I'm going to stand my ground this time.

She clears her throat. "Now, Honey, these fellows'll get in deep doo doo if they don't get you there. Doctors can't be kept waiting, and they don't know nothin' 'bout your dinner last night."

Clutching the sheets, my face all red-eyed and hot as some cornered bobcat, I am surely bristled-up for a fight.

But, I see her decide to go gentle on me. She's thinking: Coax 'em.

She signals for the men to move back with a nod of her head. One of them stands with his arms folded like a marine. The other is bent over the litter with a half-assed grin, enjoying the show.

"Honey," she says gently, "Why didn't you ring for me?"

I catch her eyes into mine and direct them toward the call button left on the table over by the door.

She spots it. "Oh," she says.

"I mean it." I whisper. "Not budging without breakfast. Got low blood. Have to eat." For emphasis, I add louder, "I'll pass out."

She stares me square in the face for three full seconds. I am not going to let go of the sheet.

Like clockwork, she turns to the tray, rips back the top of the orange juice, slaps butter and jam on the toast, scoots it in a napkin, yanks back the litter, and presents it above me,—the juice in one hand and toast in the other.

"Look, have this now, go with them. I give you my God's word that I will personally hold your tray." She states this with the air of a CEO. "When you return I'll heat it in the microwave."

I believe her.

"OK." I grab the loot.

I feel her watching me as the orderlies zip me down the hallway. I'm smugly floating in the bubble of being a bitch—one who's maneuvered a bit of control.

5:00 PM

My eyes closed, I hear the rebounding sluff of his three wide and cautious steps. They come to a halt.

Kent is here, balancing on the forward ball of his sandaled foot. *Dejavu.* This could be any summer afternoon when I am resting and he has come seeking an answer or a talk.

He approaches quietly, and upon entering my room waits in a suspended pose, studying my face to see if I am really napping.

I breathe in deeply to test whether I can detect the woodsy scent of my eldest son. The pattern of our game continues when my lips cannot keep themselves from crinkling to the same light smile that I suspect he is beaming on me.

I open my eyes as I turn my head. Wisps of long, brown hair, tinged with highlights, lace his face and neck. He is bronzed from hiking.

"Mom?" He says it in a gentle upward lilt, to be asking the question: Are you all right?

Smiling broadly, I raise my arms as an answer.

Two more steps and his hands are grasping my shoulders. Looking steadily into my eyes, he bends to kiss me first on one cheek, then the other, the way his Turkish grandmother taught him to do.

The brims of my eyes are filled. "Now, Mom, don't cry, I'm here, everything's going to be fine."

I pat the side of my bed and he sits. "I only found out yesterday when Kevin and I called Dena at the office."

To shush this apology, I say, "Your dad told me to expect you today. I've been looking for you all afternoon."

"Well, I'm here now." He brushes a strand of hair back from his face. "Dad's told me what an ordeal you've had, and none of us were with you." I look at his face for sparks of my own youth.

". . . So there I was, waiting in bed in my room, Drs. Godwin and Nolan have ordered an ambulance . . ."

Kent seem to be hanging on every word, so I continue.

"When the telephone rings and the ambulance driver finds out it's the patient answering, he asks if I'm doing OK; and I say, Fine, and he says the reason he's asking, is there's been an accident and should they go pick up this emergency before they come to take me to U.Va; and well, I'm used to important emergencies, so I say, Sure, and they say, Are you sure?"

Kent opens his mouth. I rush toward the punch line.

"So half an hour later, Dr. Godwin calls, and I answer. He says, What are you still doing there? and I tell him about the emergency, and he says, Judy, you ARE an emergency!"

Kent shakes his head. "Mom, why did that happen?"

"Seems like the ambulance people don't get many calls about Guillain-Barre syndrome and there was some misunderstanding that this was an ascending paralysis."

"I gather it's a virus that makes the immune system turn on itself," he says, pouring me a glass of ice water. He holds it while I sip through a straw.

When I have to go to the bathroom, Kent goes out and brings back a nurse, then leaves us to handle the bed pan ritual.

When he comes back, he is in high spirits. "Just phoned about my job. They want me to start waiting tables."

"What about your classes?"

"Just taking two this term. I'll work mornings and evenings."

He again sits beside me on the bed, taking my hands in his. "But the thing is, Mom, I have to go now. They want me to come in for training tonight."

"Kent, I'm so glad to have you in the same town with me."

"I understand. But I won't see you till late tomorrow. Have to sign up for classes and buy books."

Kent lifts from around his neck a leather thong strung through two silver rings with crystals attached to them. He holds them up for me to see.

"I got these out in Colorado this summer from this old Indian. They have healing power."

One is a milky-white polyhedron shape. The other is round with edges cut so that the points reflect green light.

"I can feel its vibes," I say, as he slips the necklace over my head. His green eyes sparkle.

"The love that comes with these crystals increases their power."

The magic on my neck is a symbol. "But, they are only a loan," he says, standing, "I get these back when you are well."

Like a promise.

Judy flat out loved it when June came around 'cause that's when the sour cherries got ripe. Why, she could be doing something like heaving a load of soggy towels into the dryer, and all of a sudden, she'd catch herself picturing those tangy-tart rubies in mid-air, hanging heavy in their juice, ready for the picking. Her mouth would all water up like she was getting ready to chomp down on one of her Aunt Lou's special dill pickles.

So, since sour cherries were only around for two or three weeks, Judy had to move fast when the time came. She ate 'em with salt–like with green apples. She'd just split one open, pop the seed, pour on the salt and plop it in her mouth like a gum ball. If she missed out on sour cherries, it was like summer didn't start out right.

Her big boy, Kent, was just as bad as she was about sour cherries. Maybe he got her taste-genes. He was in the fifth grade that early summer, not quite old enough yet to get shy.

Judy should've grown her own cherry tree, but never got around to it. That summer, Kent and his mom both had bloated stomachs and sore tongues from gorging on a whole bucket of cherries–ate every last one, commenced on that bucket worse than two birds, went after them until there was nothing left but juice thick as hog's blood.

Judy tossed her strawberry head like some prissy schoolgirl, and Kent grinned like a best friend. They had gone in the station wagon scouting for cherry trees. Lots of folk just let the birds have 'em.

They found a tree–just loaded–at this dead-end street down back of what used to be Cow Hill, before it was turned into asphalt, brick and birdhouse mailboxes.

Now, one thing about Kent, he didn't mind being used when I came to finding cherries. Kent, with his bright eyes against those big freckles. Mouth like a slice of watermelon. He could lean on that grin to get his way.

Judy sent Kent to that stranger's door. She didn't figure it'd look right for a grown woman to be out pan-handling for cherries. She sat in the car while Kent marched right up to the door like he was selling greeting cards to raise money for the school. Judy'd agged him on, of course. She loved being in cahoots with her kids.

Kent had to knock three times, because the TV was on inside. Could be heard clear out to the curb.

Then, the old woman came to the door. The poor soul still had her robe on, and for a second Judy felt real bad about disturbing her.

But, that feeling didn't keep, 'cause when Kent looked back at his mom, she started nodding her head for him to go on and ask. Kent later said he thought that the old lady looked at him suspiciously. Said when she poked her head out through the screen door and asked him what he wanted, he smiled big and friendly–and got right to his point. Just rared back and told the story that he and his mom had decided on–about how his mom would like to bake some cherry pies for a special person–if they could just get some fresh cherries.

Judy saw the old lady say something, then shut the door,–and Kent shrug.

She looked at her boy slinking back down the yard like a whopped dog, and looked at that tree standing there loaded down with fruits almost too ripe already–and thought she would cry. The honest thing would have been for her to go up to the door herself.

But, she shooed Kent back up.

Judy'd gotten out and eased around the car, and could see real good when the woman came to the door again. And she could tell that ole gal was mad as a wet hen. Judy was a bit startled when she heard that frail old lady yelling.

"You again! Zat your mom out there? Well, I guess you're bound to get your hands on my cherries. Why'nt you go buy some cans?"

Judy could tell Kent was trying to think fast. He said later that all that he could really think of, at first, was that old lady's hair. It was frizzen round her ears and purple as Easter basket grass, the kind that gets all over the house and you still find it under the rug in the fall.

Those two surely were determined that the old soul was going somehow to get duped out of her cherries. Anyway, she didn't care about those cherries.

Kent spoke fast. "I'll be happy to pick you some too."

The old gal just kinda scrunched up her nose and said, "I wouldn't have 'em in the house 'cause they give me toilet problems. Don't bake no pies with my sugar trouble. Let 'em rot in the rain."

That lady looked out there and saw Judy standing by the car. They weren't fooling her. Old ladies like that aren't usually taken, even if they are sick and tired. But, she for sure thought the boy's mother did want to make those pies–like any grown woman would. The old lady probably had memories.

"Take only one bucketful–no more!" Then, she slammed the door in no uncertain terms.

Later, almost at dusk, Judy and Kent put the bucket and a ladder into the station wagon, called for Kevin and Karen, and took off for Cow Hill.

They picked till dark; and though they were tempted, they only took one bucketful, brimming red–except, of course, what they all four managed to eat while picking–which was plenty for the two younger kids.

The next year, that old woman's house was being torn down and the lot bulldozed to make way for the new condos.

Later

I hoist a third forkful of mashed potatoes across the head-level tray that has been rolled so I can eat without moving my head.

The telephone dings. Two short rings. I jerk, lay the fork in my lap, roll to my left shoulder, and reach the receiver with my right hand.

"Hello?"

"Ju-dee? How ARE ye?"

Mother's voice. Like her Scotch-Irish father, she's retained that bit of Celtic–the ye, and the emphasis on the second word of this routine question. Are: to be, state of being, existence in the present.

"I'm not kicking up a storm, but I'm still in this world." I grunt and balance my upper half on my shoulder.

"Well, I should certainly hope so," she answers, adding her forced laugh, "Listen, Kevin's here and everybody wants to talk with you, but I just was anxious to see how you were."

"I'm not sure how I am," I start, wanting to re-assure her, but at the same time, wanting her worrying over me a bit. I picture them all together in my cozy kitchen.

"Now Lady," she states in her instructive tone, "You best brace up now. Nobody can help you get well faster than you yourself." She said those same words another time:

My second miscarriage, several years before Karen was born.

When I'd come home from the hospital, I'd gone upstairs to my bed and pulled the covers over my head. Postpartum depression, disappointment.

Mother had found me crying . She tried to talk but nothing would do for me. I refused her soup.

Finally, she said, "Now lady, brace up. But, if you want to collapse, you're headed in the right direction. Nobody can control that but you. Bad things happen to everybody. Some fight back and some just give in. Never you mind, though, I'll see that everything's taken care of around here. I've got two beautiful little grandsons who are waiting for supper. Just remember that it would be your collapse, yours alone."

She turned and shut the door.

As I heard her on the stairs, I cried like a baby. I thought she was cruel, heartless. After ten minutes of sobbing, I began to get angry to think that she thought I would be so weak–while she was taking over the care of my family! I'd show her!

In no time I was up on my feet and in my kitchen.

It took several years for me to realize that if she had helped me wallow in self-pity, I might have been trapped in it.

"You know how I snap back. Are you taking care of everybody, Mother? Dinner ready?"

She's dipped chicken in flour and forked it into crackling oil heated to popping in an iron skillet where she's nestled the meat, salted and peppered every piece, watched it fry furiously to a crispy-gold; then, turned each piece, lowered the heat and clopped on a lid. Her green beans, steaming, jiggling the lid on a bubbly cushion. And real mashed potatoes, and cole slaw, made like Granny's, shredded fine and tossed with vinegar dressing.

". . . wonder if there are any of the yellow tomatoes left from what I bought at the farmers' market last Saturday?" I finish asking the question with lilt—as if nothing's changed since then..

". . . got `em sliced, and chicken's almost done. Listen, `fore I go," she adds, lowering her voice as if we will gossip, "what are they saying about where you got that disease? Never heard tell of such a thing."

"They don't seem to know."

"Well, I was telling your Aunt Lou when she called this morning that I wouldn't be surprised if it wasn't something you might have picked up in California."

"Oh, Mother."

"No, it hasn't been quite two weeks since you and Karen got back. You never know what's in the air out there. I didn't think you should have gone—with Vedi overseas and all."

She waits.

I don't answer.

"Karen says the two of you took off and drove down to Mexico too, and I bet a dime you drank the water."

Why does it have to be my fault? I should have stayed home weaving like Penelope while Odysseus was out cruising the world? Maybe she thinks I should have taken her along too. But it was a trip for Karen and me.

"Mother, you say Kevin is there?"

Kevin comes on laughing. "Hey Mom—" He knows my reaction to his grandmother's prodding. Kevin shares a closeness with his Granny that I never had. She thinks everything he does is remarkable. Of course, Mother loves me—but she doesn't like my poems.

I respond to Kevin's giggling in kind. "Guess I'm here because California can't manage to keep their air clean."

"Yes, no doubt, but you could pick up a disease from just about any state in the Union these days."

"Are you sure you want to stay home this summer?"

". . . delivering pizza, minimum wage, but tips might be fine. Mom, somebody's got to get you to therapy every day once you get home."

"Therapy, who's talking about that?"

"Your doctors. They seem to think that it's going to take time to get you going,—and we most definitely have to get your muscles working so you can wash clothes, cook and scrub floors for us again us as soon as possible." He is trying to cheer me.

My head is pounding. I scoot down as flat as I am able and take in a quiet breath away from the receiver. Even though he's trying to make light of it, it's true—I need to be there managing my house. As things stand now, I'm going to be a burden. Kevin will have to give up his summer.

"Mom?"

"I appreciate it son."

His voice takes a serious tone. "Look, we're a family. It's my turn to help. You just get well, OK? Now here's Tuger."

"Hi," Karen says in a soft, sweet swing.

"How ARE you Doll Baby?" I'm trying to sound on top of it all.

"Bored," she answers, "There's nothing to do here. Missy's on vacation at the beach. Nothing to do but go walk around the mall."

"I'll be home soon and we'll rent a movie together."

"Yeah," she answers, "Wish we could go to California again."

I am surprised to hear this. She hadn't been eager to go in June. I had insisted.

"We had a wonderful trip and we'll have many more," I say. Maybe I won't be able ever again to take a trip with her.

"Is your Dad around?"

"Mom, he's been waiting to talk, but his beeper went off a couple of minutes ago. I think I just heard him drive off."

In San Francisco, we climbed Nob Hill and looked out over a blue bay. "Good for us to have this time together before you get too old," I told her. "Yeah, it's neat, I like Pat's cats, " she answered.

"Isn't the Pacific challenging?" I asked.

"It would be great with my friends," she answered.
She protruded her lips and said, "Thai tea?" She ordered another glass.

"But I made such great plans for today," I said.
"Maybe I have ideas too," she said.

"This trip isn't all that bad," she said. *"Your old pal, Pat, is cool. So were the Chinatown fortunes."*
"What did you guys do while I was in the bookstore?"
"Just cruised the streets. The neatest thing was this pots and pans band with a monkey. I gave it a quarter."

"Alcatraz! Who wants to see a spooky old prison?".
"I do. It's history."
"So go yourself."
"But it's famous, and the atmosphere—"
"Famous for what? Dying? I'll bet it stinks."

"So we fly to LA, rent a car and drive to San Diego."
"Can we get a black Fiero?"
"Sure, anything you say. Southern California is crawling with real hip young people. I got us this nice hotel."

"Nobody around this place but old people."
"Let's find ourselves a beach."
"What if an earthquake hits the beach and we fall off the edge."

"How can we be here and not see a bit of Mexico?"
"At least at this pool I can get a nice tan."
"You're the one wanted the zippy car. Now, let's use it."

"Now that was an interesting day," I was saying, while driving back up the highway from TiaJuana, both of us sunburned and greasy.
"Mom, you're turning left! Don't' you see that sign?"

"What sign?"

"We're going into the immigration check point. Citizens don't have to do that!"

"No ma'am, can't get out without a clearance," the immigration man was telling me. "

"Mom, don't you read signs? Sheeze, this place looks like a big city parking lot."

I saw how the man was taking a good look at my red hair and freckles and comparing it with Karen's olive skin and dark eyes.

"Who's the girl you got with you?"

"My daughter!"

"Sorry, ma'am, we just have to see some proper ID. Some like to smuggle in girls to work and stuff."

Slinging open the car door and slamming it, I tried to appear outraged and important. But, I had on a red and yellow Mexican shirt over a beach-dirty bathing suit. It doesn't matter, I told myself. Daddy always said to take your problems to the head man.

"Who's in charge here? I want to see the head person!"

"I'll see what I can do, but he's a busy man."

"There's big signs. Most people can read them," the head man said.

"We're from Virginia, not used to this."

"Proper ID? What did you say your name was young girl?"

"Karen."

"Had a good time out here with your mother?"

"Yes."

"Tell me about it. I need to hear you talk."

After Karen spoke about the San Diego zoo and the room service at the hotel in her southeastern drawl, and after I produced my driver's license, social security and the car rental contract, he sized us up again and said, "You know, we could hold you here for forty-eight hours. Now, get on back to Virginia and watch the signs."

Thursday, July 10, 6:30 AM

". . . hate to awaken you but Dr. Miller will be in to see you in a few minutes . . ."The nurse's voice jump-starts my batteries, sets the wheels of my mind racing as if I could take off toward some responsibility. A zing of panic spears downward from the top of my head. Where am I? What's going on? I open my eyes to the huge glaring blades of light cutting across the room. The aide is pulling open the draperies.

"Let's just get you ready," she says as she comes back toward me.

When I raise my head, the volcano awakens. "My head," I mutter.

"You still have headache?" another voice answers. Dr. Miller, with his troop, is standing at my side.

"Good morning, Judy. I hope I'm not hearing that."

"Apparently so," I answer. He is sympathetic, assuring me that the headache should go away soon, and that he is continuing my pain medication.

"Would you like to go home?"

My mouth drops. I raise forward on an elbow. "I thought I was to have an MRI today."

"To be honest," he begins, hugging my chart to his chest, "the machine is broken and they can't seem to tell me how long it's going to take to have it fixed—could be several days. In the meantime, although the testing we have done is inconclusive, your condition continues to present itself as Guillain-Barre syndrome."

"Would this MRI test be able to determine that for sure?"

The eight residents have moved closer to Dr. Miller with all of their faces screwed onto his.

"GBS," he explains, "is a condition which includes certain symptoms. Some of those symptoms are very similar to other things, which we would like to be able to rule out. We don't label GBS as a disease, because we are not certain as to the cause of it. The MRI would have given us a map of your peripheral nerve tissue, which could have been helpful in our determination of your malady."

I am rather confused but being home rebounds in my mind. "So you think I'm going to be well soon?"

"Judy, listen carefully. It could be soon. It could be late—most likely the latter. There's no way to predict how your body is going to be able to combat your condition. But one thing is sure: you need to be getting physical therapy as soon as possible. Atrophy will extend your illness." I start to ask a question, but he pushes past my interruption. "I have been in conference by telephone with Dr. Nolan in Roanoke. He is ready to set up out-patient therapy as soon as I advise him."

"You can't do any more for me here?"

"Not at the present. If necessary, you can return."

"And you don't know how long my recovery will take?"

"Nerve endings—if they heal, usually heal at the rate of one-tenth of an inch per week," he says, looking around to his flock.

After he leaves, my stomach feels like it is full of fleas. I can't imagine one-tenth of an inch, let alone calculate any length of time. I can't even guess how long are the peripheral nerves. All of those IFs— and I'm being discharged from the hospital in worse shape than when I came in—with no conclusive diagnosis—

I have to call home. Vedi will be in surgery, office this afternoon. How will I get home? Don't know where to reach Kent. Why didn't I take his number?

Dr. Miller wouldn't be sending me home unless it was safe. But he also seemed to be saying there is no way to predict what is going to happen to me.

I have to call home.

5

Homebound

Thursday, July 10, 7:00 PM

Flat on my back, I rock just enough to get a response, a soft massage from my warm waterbed. The narcotic begins to work its way into my cells like thickened oil. Breathing into my back, I lie in the dark, hearing television, arguing, teasing, ice tinkling and chairs scooting about a table prepared for a homecoming my body couldn't tolerate. Buried in the warm weight of blankets, I have no desire to rise again.

You always bounce back. You always bounce back.

These last four hours–how different than what I had imagined back in Charlottesville, where I was so eager for Kevin and Vedi, longing for that ride *back home, that sweep around Afton Mountain, perhaps a foggy-day view onto tops of trees, tires eating up the white line on the road, snipping it off into ribbons left behind us, each snip a second less of the time it would take* to get home.

They came, and the awful, head up, juggling of my body started;

and the struggle of fitting me into a wheelchair. The two nurses carped, "Why not an ambulance?"

They whisked me out the doors of the hospital.

We pushed into heat–from shadows to a shocking glare–each crack in the sidewalk a jarring eruption in my head. But worse, was the confrontation of my two-door car. Vedi's big four-door was in the shop.

The nurses were shocked: ". . . aren't going to take her in this, are you?"

And so my body had to be vaulted and stuffed into the back seat, where I, for three hours, moaned across the hump in the middle of the too-short seat, too sick to vent my anger of Vedi not hearing me when I said: I HAVE to lie flat.

The car was speeding toward home; and all the while, I was re-membering myself on that same highway, feeling hijacked then too, but going in the opposite direction.

Six days ago, I was full of apprehensions; but at least not nauseous, at least not having to stop the car, drag my head out the door three times to vomit on the side of the road, my two men watching with helplessness and fear in their faces–that they might not be able to carry out their hair-brained arrangement of getting me home.

I don't care where the rest of the world is going. I took a pill, and I am a brown dandelion blotch by the side of some road.

That trip to Poland, in 1977, was a turning point. The bus with sixty US arts educators raced over the countryside, swishing past golden blocks of mustard and fat flocks of dandelions laid against lush green.

"Sun of the earth," she noted in her journal. The stout dandelions were everywhere, on the manicured lawn of Krakow's University, groomed along with the roses of a small house along the road, and in Zakopane, the artists' village high in the Tatras.

In the early morning in Zakopane, she had gotten up and left the mountain hotel before any of the others. She needed to climb the hill, drink in the morning and make notations:

She climbs the hill with the fog, to catch the first light spark diamonds on clover, and brew mountain tea in a green fairy cup. High in an elm, a crow, oily sleek, squalls down an insult. Cuckoo retorts. They bicker across the sagging split-rail. The wind turns over, lays back the grass, then, surging upward–shakes leaves of trees like palsied palms–the snow-crested Tatra Mountains–commanding the space, looming white gods bearing shields to the sun, upstaging buttercups' gold on the green. Blades of sun touch tips with the grass. Smell of hot breads blend with black tea, careens up the hillside. She descends with daisies, two halves of tram tickets, (what hour and what time?) four crimson pebbles, a crow feather, a bone.

Until that time in Poland, she had never experienced universal one-ness, though she knew the concept.

Standing on that blackened, foot-worn soil of Auschwitz, the hush of death–still hanging in the air like invisible, wet, dingy laundry–enclosed around her. That soil beneath her feet was still full of an awful fertilizer–that soil that had been turned over and patted down by the thousands of anxious soles shuffling through days of trying to survive. The sealed display of the relics of them remained: thousands of shoes, boxcar loads of hair, eye glasses, utensils of the past, waiting in the present for some explanation. That reality had given her three dreams where corpses with white skulls and blue holes for eyes had come to her, saying, "When shall we have peace?"

And, those children in the classrooms. Her group had been the first Americans allowed to speak with teachers and students. The Poles, with their muted tenacity, had hated the Communist rule. In her journal, she had smuggled back the determination set in their lips, their love of the earth, their exchange of words through sign-language. She had called it her Smuggled Seeds, had plucked a handful of a huge bristle of dandelions and thrust them in her jeans. The Poles and the Holocaust victims were dandelions: dried seeds, like ash gone to green, yellow, hardy, insistent, everywhere, survivors, not weeds but flowers.

She had squirmed that day on the bench in that classroom at Krakow University, listening to a boring recitation on the history of Polish music. There were five other adventuresome friends in the group who sneaked out with her.

"Where shall we go?" one asks. She had told them she had seen school children in blue uniforms go into a building. The six located the building. The one from Oregon, a dancer with Polish heritage, pretended to be an interpreter when they strode into the principal's office.

"We are Americans, here today to observe your classrooms," he announced. Then, the nervous scurry, the tea, the apology for the misunderstanding. Oh, they knew Americans were on campus, but somehow they had not been informed they would be observed. Finally, the skinny lady with the salt and pepper beehive advised them: "We have a rehearsal underway for the spring concert, if you would forgive any mistakes, we would be pleased to have your presence."

At the rehearsal, seventh and eighth grade students sang six-part a capella counterpoint, not only traditional songs, but tone-poems in mid-air: waves lapping on a shore, foot steps, a gun shot and running, a bird lifting wings from water. Dr. Ciuraba, the conductor, said, "Just call me Joe," and invited them to his home.

It was forbidden to go away from the tour, but they went.

His wife must have spent all afternoon making those artistic little sandwiches. After dinner, Joe had entertained with verse on verse of Negro Spirituals, memorized in English.

"I understand restriction, but my heart is free," he said.

Friday, July 11, 10:00 AM

Flinching from the sound of a steady knocking in a muffled roar, I awaken. It takes me a few seconds to remember: I'm home,–home, where from the deck or through windows, I can look out and over to Catawba Mountain, Poor Mountain, and Cahas Knob, where there's patches of hillsides with romantic names like the Occaneechi Orchards. Watching the breathing of those old Blue Ridge giants should rejuvenate me.

Light peeps through the centerfolds of the heavy draperies. It is morning, but the digital figures on the clock are turned from me. The small red glare spears into the dusky room. I attempt to roll over. My hips and legs won't move with the rest of me. On an elbow, I stretch my neck: Ten o'clock. That pill really knocked me out last night.

I lie back on the pillow, relishing the familiar noise of my dishwasher's waterfall. A lid's not secure in the rack. They should stop the machine and fix the lid so it won't keep knocking. The television is on: cartoons. Karen will be in pajamas, one leg slung over the back of the couch, slurping cereal, her eyes glued to the tube.

"Better come with me and see if we can get her up." Mother's voice in the foyer. Her hand is on the doorknob. I prepare to smile, manage a hoarse, "Hi." Mother stops at the desk.

"Well," she answers, "You been awake long?"

"Just woke." I swallow on a dry throat. She stares at me, likely wondering whether I'm better or worse this morning. Pondering the same, I envision throwing back the covers, bounding from bed, and bouncing into the sun.

Mother prances past the foot of the bed to open the drapes.

After she calls Karen for the third time, my daughter tears herself away from cartoons and runs in barefooted, the tail of her shorty pajamas flouncing at her slender hips, makes a dive onto my wheelchair, and propels it to my side.

"Welcome home!" she yells, flashing a perfect set of teeth. She bats her dark eyes. "What's wrong?"

"Nothing, just looking. You've grown since I've been gone." She screws her face into that "Oh Mom" look. Seems like I've been away for months.

Karen uncovers my legs, surprised to see my "gladiator" shoes. "You have to wear those things in bed?"

"My feet would get tangled in the sheets without them." They didn't seem so odd in Charlottesville.

"How's your head, Mom?" I hadn't noticed, but the pounding is gone.

I'm a bit frightened by the way they are going about trying to get me up, Karen tugging at my hips and Mother on my shoulders. My words snap at their hands. "Hold it! I'll tell you what I need you to do!" They wince.

I struggle to raise my shoulders but my legs weigh a ton.

"Maybe if you'd just let me–" Mother offers, again taking my shoulders.

Karen steps in close, wraps her arms around my back, and they heave together. When I'm almost sitting, Mother stuffs a pillow behind me.

"Just let me rest a minute."

"Judy," my seventy-one year old mother advises, "You're going to have to let us carry you."

My face flushes when they again reach for me. "I said wait," I say in a choked voice, "You have to let me see what I can do for myself."

What if my bones got broken? It was easy doing toilet at the hospital. Nurses are trained for care-taking. What if I'm helpless from now on? But, my bladder feels like it's going to burst.

"OK, let's go again, get me to sitting. Slowly."

Cautiously, they bend me forward. Mother steadies me as Karen hauls my legs over the side. We make clumsy attempts that fail to get me into the wheelchair even though my waterbed is even with the chair.

"Let me grab its arm," I say.

"And balance with your other arm," Karen says.

"And we'll heave you off so you can drop onto the seat," Mother adds. She runs her fingers through her unruly champagne and gray bob.

When my butt hits the chair, it rolls.

"Lock the wheels first!" I scream, "–If I fall and break something–!"

To get onto the commode, I slide down the chair's side, grab the toilet, push against the chair, and pivot over.

The glory is short-lived. I have peed into my nightgown. It oozes onto the floor. Karen and Mother rush back into the bathroom. Their clamor turns to giggles.

"Mom, you might want to pull up your gown before you do that," Karen says. She is breathless, doing a little dance, "You didn't do anything worse, did you?"

"What's all this noise about?" Kevin sleepily calls from the hall.

Karen darts out to tell her brother what their mother has just done.

My head again. I don't think I'm going to be able to continue being nice. I wish I could jump in the car and take off down the Parkway.

Hell, I can't go anywhere. I grimace back at the puffy face staring at me from the mirror: old, frumpy.

"Now, brace up, this is nothing. Remember, you've birthed three kids, why, you just slough off a little problem like this," Mother says. All the while she consoles, she is pulling my dripping gown from beneath my butt, then lifting it over my arms and head.

"I'll be happy to give you a sponge bath."

"No, thanks. I might as well smell like I feel."

Mother doesn't answer, takes another gown from a peg on my bathroom door, and lets it fall over my torso. I am an invalid, it seems. I am an invalid.

I pass by the stalls of flowers at the Farmers Market. There's not a lot on the long row of tables today. Maybe because it's Monday, the local produce hasn't yet hit full force, so I quickly move down the street, scanning the assortment as I go.

At one table, I almost buy, for ten bucks, a handmade decorated wooden rabbit. The toothy thing is fetching and tall as a three-year old kid, but I don't choose to lug it around today. Besides, "bunny day" is a month away. Not a bad idea for a gift, though.

I turn to retrace my steps to the dark purple pansies, knowing that they will look like velvet on my patio, and be tough enough to withstand a few more cold spells once this weather's tease is past. Then, there at the side of the Bent Mountain huge heads of cabbage and thick tongues of spinach, just picked this morning, is a tin bucket piled to the brim with creasys, the green lacy stars.

I pluck a cluster by one strand and study on it.

"They're good for you," the man in the overalls says. He probably thinks a city girl like me doesn't know what to do with it.

"Oh yeah," I answer, "when I was a girl of six or eight, I thought we ate poor people's food—stuff like beech nuts, huckleberries, pinto beans and creasy greens. Years later, I found out that we were picking health food."

The balmy sun and the bit of the wild fields of my childhood, dangling from my fingers like a frowzy wig, takes me across a damp meadow where I hunted the creasy with the fervor of Easter egg hunting: My Mamma's rich red hair glows in the spring sun. She is off a ways from me. Both us fill paper pokes. In rhythm, we stoop. She has taught me how to cut off the tender doily greens just above the roots. We are harvesting together.

Mamma and I will later wash our greens, tops and bottoms, until all the dirt and beads of mud are gone; and then, for supper, she'll boil them down with bacon. There, in the meadow, I mimic how she methodically clutches, pulls and collects.

Mamma's hands are waitress' hands. Her fingers splayed, they are trays that can tote three glasses at once. On this afternoon, her freckled fingers have showed me how to carry a sharp tool. I'm careful to hold the point away from me as I work. Mamma told me, "Act like you have the sense you were born with, and you can learn."

Anyway, I'm too used to rocks and holes in the ground to trip. She has entrusted me with one of her good paring knives. She is not worried that I can't handle this task.

"It's great that you can just wheel yourself right up to the kitchen table," Kevin says between bites of cornflakes. I nod back, chewing on a piece of toast. I'm making a mental note to get myself a pillow so I will be sitting at an adult level.

"How about I pour you a glass of orange juice," Mother says to my back.

I shake my head, No. My stomach is not feeling so good. I push away my plate of half-eaten egg as the telephone rings.

Karen grabs the phone off the wall. "Hi Kent! No, she's not asleep. Right here. Here, at the table, having breakfast."

Karen gives me the phone.

"How's it going Mom?"

"It's good to be home."

"How's the pain?"

I'm able to tell him the headache is better, but my legs have developed an aching that is radiating up into my hips.

"Wow—I know you might not think so, Mom, but Dad says any feeling, including pain, is a good sign."

I take a pill. The aching's increasing. Maybe because Kent asked. Clicking back the lock on the wheel, I swing my chair around.

"Want me to take you into the living room?" Kevin says.

I glance up at him. His thick auburn hair, still wet from the shower, folds in wisps at his neck. Hard to believe he was once a blonde.

"I can take myself." I answer with more tension in my voice than I intend. The seasick nausea ebbs over me.

The telephone rings. This time it is my textbook writing partner, Rebekah. She is also the director of Hollinsummer, where I should be teaching this week.

"No, no, don't worry about your class. We got a replacement last Sunday afternoon, and the students just love her."

Great.

"No one is irreplaceable," I say, clearing my throat.

"Ah, now, it's just lucky Katherine was available."

After I say goodbye, a queasy sensation sends me rolling toward my bathroom. I'm going to throw up. I can still do that for myself, from the wheelchair.

"We have to leave for your therapy in an hour, so you better let us help you get ready." Kevin is calling after me.

Before he finishes his sentence, I know that I am not going to any therapy today. Maybe never.

Saturday, July 12, 1:OO PM

Mother takes my plate away from the table and pauses. "Do you want more coffee?"

I decline. "Think I'll go back to bed for a while." I catch her tight knit of the brow and lips.

"You better watch sleeping so late. You're gonna start exercising at the hospital, aren't you?"

She waits.

I look away.

"Kevin's staying home this summer to help you get back on your feet."

I throw her the bored look like Karen gives me.

Mother goes to the sink, drops the plate into the suds, and begins scrubbing. Why does she insist on doing that when we have a dishwasher? Probably thinks she's saving water. She's never gotten over THE Depression. I like my dishes sterile. I inhale audibly, then let out a short puff.

"I never waste time with that. Just stick them in the machine."

"I kind of enjoy doing it." She rinses a bowl and stacks it onto the rack.

A mild agitation starts to move into my arms and chest. Why does she always have to do things her way when she is in my house? I study the objects on the open counter dividing the kitchen and the great room. She's rearranged the crystal bowls and vases I keep on it, and added two different sets of salt and pepper shakers, plus two jars of olive oil and a pitcher of vinegar. Looks a bit tacky. I did things her way in her kitchen for twenty years.

She glances back at me. "Did you want something else? There's tea in the icebox if you want some."

"It's a refrigerator, Mother, a refrigerator." I wheel past her.

"And I really do think it's more efficient," I call over my shoulder, lacing it with as sweet a tone as I can muster, "to do the dishes in the machine."

"Well—do tell!" she answers.

Gladys has always been a walker, but when you grow up in coal towns back of the Kanawah River you either learn to walk hollers or else you don't go nowhere.

Her courtin', as a young girl, consisted of trekking down the railroad tracks on Sunday after church—three or four of her sisters trailing along a safe distance behind. Her mother didn't believe in giving the seven girls she had on hand too much freedom; and she was right, raised all those girls, and not a one ever got in the family way before marriage.

She stands and moves toward the bathroom, stretching out the soreness from the night, thinking: Good legs run in the family. Although there are the broken veins; but those came from child-bearing and all those years of running up and down the table aisles.

Was not easy to take off every day and leave three kids. But work was scarce and the children's daddy couldn't seem to bring in enough to ever get ahead. Shouldn't have rushed off and gotten married in the middle of the depression. Seems it hung on longer in West Virginia than anywhere else.

She removes the partial-plate from the plastic box by the sink, rinses it and fits it in her mouth. She looks at herself in the mirror and chuckles as she tells the reflection, "Now, why are you thinking about those hard times?"

But, she continues: After the war. Had gotten it in our heads we could be farmers. Spent what little we had saved on that 50-acre eight 'n plum— eight miles back and plum out in the country. Back up that carved-out bend in Teays Valley. Wasn't much there then.

My man, J.G., walked ten miles every day up the river to Nitro to the rubber plant, leaving me with three small youngins and land that needed more attention than I could tend to.

Was two miles on those ruts and rocks out the way to the Mangus' store. And you had to go whether there was mud knee-deep or not. Seemed you never had proper boots to wade through snow. Had to drag the kids along; and the youngest was hardly walking. Took a half-day.

Only made a few hundred dollars on that farm when we sold it. And glad enough for that, just to get out from between those dark hills. Interstate runs right down the middle of it now.

She sighs, as she does every time she thinks of what kind of money that would mean to her. But, she grins to think of them holding onto that land for the twenty years it took the state to decide they needed it. "No need to think about what never was," she whispers. A lot of opportunity just slipped away.

Mom and Dad are both gone. That old white house still stands on I-64,—not our farm, but the house where Judy was born. When J.G. and I lived with Mom and Dad.

That was some winter, February snow up to the swing out back. Gladys sees herself with long red hair, huge with pregnancy: Her time had come and she's downstairs in the front bedroom so as to be near the big fireplace in the living room across the hall.

Sent J.G. out to get the doctor earlier. Watched how he hunched his shoulders into the wind as he left the yard, making deep holes in the smooth snow. He'd be in luck to get a hitch-hike.

Had such a hard time with Jon—twenty-one hours of labor, then almost bled to death. Didn't want to take chances.

But then, a big pain. Got up onto the cold bare floor and trekked over to the enamel pot, thinking I had to go bad. Sometimes you do before labor sets in.

Judy almost came in the chamber pot, for sure—if it hadn't been for Mom and Aunt Mag to carry me to the bed.

By the time J.G. got back with that doctor, there wasn't anything to do but take the afterbirth.

Sometimes folks have it hard and they're struggling so to just survive that they don't even know till later how hard it really is. And that's a blessing, 'cause if they did, they probably wouldn't have the strength and good humor to see it through.

That Judy was in a hurry to get into this world; and she never did slow down a bit, till this disease hit her. Mom thought she ought to be named Maggie, but J.G. was sweet on Miss Garland.

I sit in a cloud of gloom, skimming over my bedroom wall of pictures. Kin from both sides of the family. Some dead and gone, some grown. All special. Why am I making such a scene out of things that do not matter? My body—worse, my spirit—is falling apart. Where's the strong adult I was going to be—the one who would get me through all this?

Wheeling straight on, I'm facing the side of my waterbed. After I flip back the wheel lock, I sit a moment, thinking. I don't know who I am anymore. My kids are taking care of me, I've lost my jobs. I wipe my cheek on my shoulder. I don't want them to see me cry. They're always bopping in and out my door.

Brace up. It's not THAT bad. At least, this chair lets me go to the toilet alone–and it gives my daughter a toy to play with: Karen last night–wheeling around the corner of the dining table, pulling the breaks and spinning like she was on a bumper car ride.

Getting into bed can't be that hard. I begin to lift and hoist my heels one at a time onto the side of the bed. Finally, I roll the wheels until the chair is flush with the bed, lock it and grunt and pull until I'm in–shaped like a pretzel. Inching around on the sheet, I straighten out.

"Judy?"

I didn't hear Vedi coming. He bends to kiss my cheek; then steps to my side, grinning at me as he undoes his shirt button and removes his tie.

Sitting on the bed, facing me, he takes my hand and speaks softly. "Sweetheart, you have to get to therapy."

I cringe. "I have pain, and I'm so tired all the time, you all don't understand." He turns my face to him.

"You have to stop taking the Darvon. Now wait,–I know the doctor gave it to you, and I do understand you have pain; but it is slowing you down more."

"How can I deal without it?"

"Do you ever want to be independent again?"

My mouth drops open. What a stupid question!

"You can't take a narcotic and therapy at the same time."

Sunday, July 13, 10:00 PM

New-age "lost in space" music floats out of the radio.

". . . for your listening pleasure," croons Jeff Hunt's rusty-raw-silk voice, "Here at eleven ohh-five, Sunday night, on your number-one public radio station–WVTF . . ."

I adjust my shoulders into my pillow and push the covers off my chest, relishing the cool breath of central air. It sounds like a constant rain washing over my skin.

The music circles and spreads in long fingers, smoothes across the tip of my eyelash, the nub of my nose. It reaches past the amber light from the lamp and joins the muffled sounds of my husband as he bathes in the bathroom. I relish the steamy scent of his soap, a mixture of raisins and peppermint.

The shower shuts off. Now, I know how he's bending with the thick, pink towel bunched in his hands. He gently rubs the glistening from his hair-streaked thighs, his boyish wet hips, his blooming abdomen. I wonder if he will shave.

The radio's cool melodic fingers are stroking tension away in a moist air, careening on my collar bone, and gliding playfully beneath my gown, cupping my breasts. I crave this touching. My body moves with the airwaves. My feet are moonlight, my hair is rain.

"Are you asleep?" he whispers. I open my eyes. Vedi's standing by the bed, one hand ready to turn back the covers.

"Oh no, Sweetie, just listening."

He throws back the covers, puts a knee up to get in, and pauses. "Do you mind if I read for a few minutes—I want to review a procedure for surgery tomorrow."

I hesitate. I want his attentions. He is reaching for a book on his night stand, but stops his hand as he sees my reaction. "Oh, I'm sorry, you must be tired, I can do it in the morning."

His weight jostles the waterbed. My back is enjoying the caress of riding the ripples he creates under me. He settles into his pillows, lying on his back.

Strange, but it feels awkward. I've been home several days, and we have not touched each other except for him to help me get up or down, or to kiss like sister and brother. I sense that Vedi, too, is feeling needy.

He turns onto his side. "You're dressed-up tonight."

I'm tickled that he noticed I'm wearing something besides my nightshirt.

"I don't mind if you read. I just wanted to talk a little bit," I say.

He reaches over and puts his hand on my shoulder, then skims it down my arm, his soft fingers lightly touching my breast. How are the two of us supposed to deal with my paralysis? Everything has changed.

I am a crippled Handicap. Can I ever be sexual again? Would I feel anything? Would he want me?

His eyes are skating in mine. "What are you thinking about? Worried about going to therapy tomorrow?"

I chuckle. "Something like that."

"I know what you need," he whispers, grinning.

Has he asked my doctor about this?

"You need a little activity," he states quietly.

I nod my head. I am thinking how I really MUST look sexy lying here at this minute weighed flat by blankets, unable to even turn with these "gladiators" strapped on–missing one-half of my body.

"I've become useless." Turning my neck, I study his response. He is smiling with his lips closed.

"I feel terrible that you have been gone a month, and now you're home and we can't even be–normal."

He reaches a hand to my head and plays with my hair.

"We'll adjust to everything," he says, "but, like I said, first step is physical therapy."

Touching his chin, I urge him to lean over and kiss me. He has not shaved.

She had joined the Sixty's Revolution in her own way by leaving home. Until then, she had been commuting to Marshall University for almost three years from ten miles out of Huntington. When she turned twenty-one and Daddy still wouldn't let her date, without a fight, it was long past time to break free. She had finances: Worked three days a week at Anderson's department store.

She had been hanging around the dorm, where she had spent her first night on her own. They only charged five dollars a night, but she couldn't stay more than a couple of days. She had a feeling that something was already worked out for her, somewhere. She was waiting for the appropriate place to make itself known, as if God Himself had taken a personal interest in her situation.

Actually, she was in quite a casual mood about homelessness, quite expectant. For the first time in her life, time was in her own hands. Not accountable to anyone, she had wings; and it was spring. When she told her friend, Pat said, "I can't believe you got up the nerve to take the step to freedom." She was curious and full of admiration that Pat had become a neat kind of artist-hippie. She might as well become one, too.

Meeting him was the result of the whim of moving in with those three new friends. That was some place: Up a dim narrow wooden stairway, stain-worn at the center from hurrying feet, where the walls were a yellowed collage of hand prints, carbon smears, smoke, sweat, donuts' sugar smudge, and patches scarred by unsteady or jostled shoulders. Up this flight of stairs, she went, each step creaking, announcing her arrival. And, then, in through the high-ceilinged kitchen where pop bottles clustered at the sink, waiting to be returned for deposit, iron pot on the stove soaking in suds, smelling slightly of burnt beans, linoleum floor of nondescript colors with permanent scuffs from stove to sink. The refrigerator was overwhelmed with papers and notes held on by magnetic clips and badges. The white door's main purpose seemed to be to support an extended hanger of dresses, skirts and blouses.

The gals had told her to hang her jacket on the knob, and welcomed her to the pad.

The main room was painted completely black, like the inside of a coal box. In one corner, there was a roughly-built bar, made of old lumber, also painted black and decorated with long strips of plastic multicolored beads. A group of wine and beer bottles cloistered at one end of its counter, all emptied. A gray fish net billowed across the ceiling. Around one side of the room was an assortment of large pillows, which served alternately as a bed and a social seating arrangement. Candles, burned down into lumpy globs in saucers, were scattered about the room, and ashtrays, pilfered from hotels, were full of the usual stems and charcoal. Incense burnt in a brass crock in the far corner.

The only bedroom contained a double bed that took up most of the space. The two who turned in first went to sleep in there.

Clothes draped every available hook or handle.

From the stereo behind the bar, Joan Baez strummed and wailed a soft protest. Immediately, she had liked it all.

"Where do I sleep?" she had asked; and they had said, "No problem."

If one could sleep in the pillowed corner, two could as well; and she had called Jon to bring her clothes from home.

She was making $25. a week. Her share of fifty, a month's rent, and groceries split four ways would be managed–with a bit to burn; and ten percent she would tithe–just so God would keep the other end of the bargain.

She met him that first afternoon when he came in with her new blonde roomy, whom he had met while treating the blonde's uncle in the C and O Hospital down the street, where he lived as a second-year surgical resident.

He was in white tennis shorts and had a far-out foreign accent and the cutest thighs. She told him so when he sank into the cushion next to her. He much later confessed that he thought she was making a sexually aggressive move; but when he studied her, he was confused. She was trying to be cool, not knowing quite how to act in the surroundings, not wanting to stand out like a sore thumb, yet thrilling with the air of adventure.

The blonde was a majorette. He liked parading the blonde with the great body around the residents' quarters. Their friendship did not move beyond his reading the blonde's palm and a few long kisses. The kisses, the blonde had recommended.

Many's the night he would call after ten, saying, "Meet me half-way?" and she'd slip on tennis shoes and skip out the door. In 1962, There was no danger in the darkness on those streets.

Half-way, there he'd come, perhaps still in his surgical greens or the white jacket he wore for rounds. They'd sometimes sit on the damp fire-escape at the back of her apartment until early morning, listening to the plant across the alley with its steel bruising steel like a clatter of crashing plates; or they would walk among street lamps, and the musty smell of spotted dust and gutter stench, from where the rain had sprinkled a bit.

On the honeymoon in Washington, DC–all their clothes had been stolen out of the car while they were in a Greek restaurant, where he had taken her their first night there, to show her what Turkish food was like– "only better." The police were no help, had only bawled them out for being stupid; and informed them they'd never see their clothes again.

He'd bought her a new coat instead of a diamond, and she'd bought him a tux to wear at the wedding–

"Who gives this woman?" "I give myself away."– in the campus chapel. Though they had little money, it took them no time to decide not to be down about that theft; and proceed to have a fun week, wearing the same clothes every day.

After, it became a good tale at parties, that ended with saying, "Since all our clothes were stolen, we had to spend the honeymoon in bed."

That twenty-first year, her feet became quicksilver through a magic hourglass. She thought that nothing could ever hold her back again.

6

Dancing On Pews

Monday, July 14, 10:30 AM

"You're going to dump me out!" I am shifting like a sack of potatoes. My fingers claw the arms of the wheelchair. The small step from the front stoop to the sidewalk looms before me like a terrifying cliff.

Kevin pulls the chair back.

"Take it easy Mom." His voice is tremulous. "I just have to get the hang of handling someone in a wheelchair," he adds. My pulse pounding into my neck.

"I'm not ready for this," I answer.

"OK Mom, then be ready," Kevin replies, with an edge of uncertainty. My son is built like Vedi, short and not particularly muscular. "Granny!" Kevin calls over his shoulder through the open door.

Karen appears in front of me, bracing her hands against the arm rests of the chair. The two of them ease me down onto the walk while Mother councils from the doorway, "Oh Lordy, Lordy, watch where you're going with her."

Two minutes later, my chair and I are wedged into the open door of the Thunderbird.

"You're going to have to get the door open more than that!" Kevin says in frustration.

"It won't open any wider!" Karen retorts.

"Then how am I going to lift her into the car?" Kevin snaps.

I lower the side of my chair. It is parallel to the car's front seat.

Kevin tries to lift me from under my arms. This cargo won't budge.

"Just leave me alone and let me tumble my torso sideways over onto the seat."

Then, I lie floundering like a beached whale.

"I'm sorry, Mom," Karen says, giggling, stepping in to pick up my feet while Kevin pushes my hips. I clench the rim of the seat as they heave and shove until, inch by inch, they stuff me inside.

"Maybe she should rest a few more days," Mother mumbles, shaking her head.

My sentiments exactly.

Karen drags me upright and snaps on my seat belt. Kevin loads the chair into the trunk. I could easily vomit but the thought of being strapped in, the heat, and the clean-up deters me.

Kevin slides into the driver's side, eyeing me with a tense smile. His golden hair has fallen around his face like a cherub's. "Ready?" he asks, then adds, "Dad's meeting us."

I strain a grin, distracted by a new sensation in my left ear:–ECH-OES, like I've developed an ear within an ear. My head feels somehow dislocated from my body.

Voices and machines clamor around me. To my left, there is a row of high tables with mat tops. White curtains on rungs separate each. Treadmills and exercise machines are scattered at the center. Two doorways open at the far end of the wide, high-ceilinged room. It's like a gym. People of all ages, dressed in shorts or workout clothes, are using equipment, alone or with help. Surely I don't belong in this group. I am relieved to see no familiar face. It is so complicated to explain what has happened to me.

"So this is our new patient," someone says.

The chipper voice belongs to a medium-built, dark-haired woman in a lab coat and navy pants. Vedi is standing behind her. She is holding a clipboard. As she waits for me to answer, her face is one big smile.

"My name is Ella, I'm your therapist."

Vedi blows me a kiss as he's out the door.

Ella signals with a finger and a lean man in a blue uniform hurries across the room.

"Judy, this is Al. Al–our new patient. We're just going to go over here where we can chat a bit before we begin," Ella says, as Al pushes me to the other side of the nurses' station.

When I have given her my history, I ask, "How long do you think it will take me to walk again?"

She pushes the short, thick curls back from her face. "I'd be lying if I told you I could say. We don't often see patients with GBS, but I have been working with a patient who's had it for over a year."

I gasp. She lays a hand on the arm of my chair. "But he was paralyzed all the way up–head and all. Was on a respirator. You have use of your arms. He still can't feel his feet."

I don't say anything. "He is doing quite well," she adds reassuringly, "Gets around on a cane."

Will I ever get around on a cane?

Ella stoops and begins to inspect my legs. "What do you have on your feet?"

"I call them my "gladiator shoes." Ella studies them with curiosity.

"They are hard to sleep with," I add.

"We'll have foot braces made so you can work here."

Ella gets Al again. Immediately, I'm wheeled to the end of the room and positioned at metal parallel bars.

I glance across the gym. An old lady inches her way between two such bars that extend about six yards.

"We have to find out what muscles you CAN operate," Ella says, locking my chair into place.

What is expected? Surely they don't think I can move as well as that old lady.

Al is behind me, his hands on the back of my chair. Ella straddles my feet. A tightening ache at the base of my skull flows down my spine.

"You must fully trust me," Ella says, leaning over me, putting her arms around my waist and clasping her hands at my spine. Al digs his hands into my armpits. Ella's breath huffs past my right ear.

"What are you going to do with me?"

"Reach out and take hold of the parallel bars with both of your hands," she answers.

As I reach, I feel an uncomfortable closeness of four smashed breasts.

"Relax, and get a good grip," she says.

On the count of three, I am yanked from my seat to wobble in the air like a goofy Jack-Out-of-the-Box while the room goes whooshing.

"I am going to break my ankles!"

"You're not going to do that. Trust me!"

I feel heavy, bloated, trapped.

"When I ask, take a step as I pull you forward."

I groan. Is she nuts?

"Don't worry, we've got you–" She is panting.

Ella steps backwards. I am a blob leaning onto her with Al's hands hooked under me. Was I really ever one who could zip onto center stage?

Ella steps backwards, and my legs and feet drag forward an inch or two as we take two more heaves and lurches. My feet are mounds of clay. "Ahhh,ooo," I hear myself saying, my ears pulsating with that echoing, as the air turns to violet and lime pansies, and my face seems to melt down into my neck.

Finally, they lower me back into the chair. Circling around my head, the pansies suck like guppies.

"You have done more than I expected. You took four steps!"

I am wheezing. "You're placating. No STEPS."

"But you did, didn't she Al?"

He bends around and nods his head.

This is disgusting.

"I'm not going to tolerate being treated like a baby! I still have some dignity." I want to scream.

Ella stoops and grips my arms. "Look, the last thing I would do is to placate," she says, looking me in the eyes. "I would never baby you. How dare you insult me as a professional." Her black eyes sparkle. "You'll have to re-evaluate your standards in here. Those steps were equal to running a race."

After a rest, we do the strange struggle again. After the first lurch, my stomach surges into my throat. "I'm going to throw up and faint!"

At once, Ella and Al lift me up into their arms as if they had re-hearsed it.

They are carrying me like a log. I am swallowing hard between deep breaths.

Ella is chirping, "Not on my shift!"

My body descends to a smooth landing on a mattress on the floor.

I close my eyes and the undulating dark pansies swim inside. The next thing I know, Al is applying a cold towel to my forehead.

I pull the towel down so that it covers my eyes. The sound of Ella's voice reverberates. "You see, the quickest way to get action around here is to threaten throwing up."

Mamma went right out and bought my sixth grade cheerleader skirt. But why didn't she realize that cheerleaders' skirts are suppose to flare out when they jump up and turn in the air? Those big pleats.

Anyway, it's navy like it's supposed to be. Nancy has a black skirt, but at least it's full.

But, the main thing is–I made the squad. Then, that stuck up Susan said, "Your skirt isn't appropriate," right in front of everybody, and I said, "This is the way I like it."

Can't take the chance of asking Mamma to take it back. She might not have time to bother. Might just decide I don't need to have it all that bad.

Can't do the split either. Susan can, with her long black hair falling back over her shoulders, and her mamma being the girl scout leader, and them not able to make room for one more. Who cares? I'm a Campfire Girl, anyway, now.

I allow myself to imagine being able to fling myself up into air and split down onto the center of the gym with everybody saying how cute we are at half-time while the boys' basketball team takes breaks and waves to us as they go off the floor.

Truth is, people probably say, "Gee, she is awkward, lucky she made the squad." They'll never know I give it a thought, from the way I jump, zip and yell with more energy than anybody and giving them that zinging smile I practice in the bathroom mirror.

Mamma and Daddy don't care about the games. But I'm buying penny candy when I can, putting it away in one of the lower drawers in the kitchen; and I'm gonna surprise them on Easter morning with a basket for both of them.

No one can say I only think of myself, no one can say I need to be treated special.

Wednesday, July 16, 3:00 PM

Karen is sitting on the balcony, sunning her legs, with her heels balanced on the railing. Mother's downstairs taking her afternoon nap, and I'm stretched out here in the great room on the couch, supposedly resting from this morning's therapy. My mind is filled with today's experiences: Electrodes hooked to my calves, electricity buzzed through my feet.

"Attempt movement each time you feel the shock." Weights strapped to my ankles. "Lift each foot for ten minutes using abdominal and hip muscles."

Al, lifting me like a Barbie Doll from that table to the motorized table where they strapped me down and raised it, my feet on a shelf.

Ella, pushing the button and my head continuing upward.

My ears popped. Was afraid of falling off–face down. The floor looked a block away.

Half way up, she paused. "Get used to the rise in elevation. You are securely strapped. Just relax and enjoy the ride."

She loosened the straps at the knees.

"How can I bend my knees? They'll fall out."

"You can't fall. Just let yourself hang."

If I don't, this spectacle will be prolonged. Perpendicular to the floor.

"You are putting weight on your feet. Aren't you proud?"

I pulled a smile against the force of gravity and put my faith in the strength of straps, and hung like a human billboard.

Karen thinks I'm asleep here on this couch. I watch her through the sliding glass doors. She has positioned her chair so the sun will cut across the lower half of her body. She's oiled up to the thighs, trying to keep her tan. Crows fly to and from the top of a patch of trees on the bank, moving randomly, with perfect freedom. Even though it's hot, a breeze is blowing across the hill.

The two of us haven't had a real conversation since I came home from Charlottesville. Karen's keeping a distance. Or maybe it's me, feeling so displaced. She's growing up, doesn't need me hanging around her all the time. She must wonder what to do for me, but I can tell that she doesn't want to deal with my complaints. I ask her if she's OK. "Naturally." I quiz Mother. "Karen doesn't talk much."

There's an awkward pretending going on in the family—as if everything is going to be fine—when we're all expecting something to suddenly shatter, stepping around that proverbial elephant stretched out in the middle of the floor, acting as if it's not there, wondering what it's going to do next.

I don't like feeling out of control.

Karen's been helpful this week, like this morning, with my bathing. I can sense that she's wary, like me.

I keep having terrifying moments when I think the paralysis is advancing. Then I stop and make myself realize it isn't. But it could.

I wonder if Karen keeps remembering coming home and finding me on the floor that morning.

"Tugger is scared," Kevin told me today, coming back from therapy. "She told me that after you described how the bottoms of your feet feel gritty, like they are caked with sand, she went outside, made some mud, and let it dry on her feet."

I was very touched to imagine my young imp doing that experiment, in her own secret way.

Kevin reached across the seat and laid a hand on my arm. "Karen told me that she did that to try to feel what you are feeling. When the mud dried, she couldn't move the bottoms of her feet without cracking it. She asked me what I thought it would it be like not to feel at all. She said that she doesn't know how you can stand it."

Karen always did have her own individual way of dealing with situations.

By the time Karen was three, she was a textbook case of a tomboy–from following around her two heroes, who played soccer, swam on teams and went to school. Not only was she the smallest one in the family, but she felt that she had been deprived of the handy piece of gear that the boys had, which made it easier to go to the bathroom; and she held me directly responsible for somehow not having given her one.

"I'm going-a get one I grow up," she'd said, tossing her mop of unruly black hair. "–and ride big sickles un play pee-nanno re-sitles."

Naturally, determined as she was, Karen had already figured out how to make do with what she lacked. She had developed a knack of how to pee–dead-center into the middle of the commode–without sitting down: Spread the feet, arch back like the boys, and aim that perfect arc. She was full of herself that she had achieved the admiration of her brothers for this feat. Her snapping black eyes were not going to miss a trick. It was just a matter of keeping up.

There I was–in full swing with the Christmas spirit, with cookbooks all over the kitchen table. I had called the boys in from the back yard. Karen heard us talking, and wandered in from the sun room, where she was giving a Barbie a ride in a dump truck.

"What do you like best? That's all you have to decide," I told them. Kent was sitting in the yellow leather booth with his elbows on the table, studying three books that I had opened.

"I like the chocolate peanut kind," Kevin said over his shoulder. He was rummaging through a drawer near the sink.

"Yeah, but I'm not so sure they are really Christmassy, and if you are going to take these to school for your class, you want them to look right," Kent said, bending down toward one of the books.

Karen moved around to the other side of the booth; then, she crawled in and scooted halfway up onto the table, jutting her head over the Kent's book.

"Tug, move, we have to read these recipes," Kent said, giving her a little push on the head. She slid back and scowled.

"If you want them to look seasonal, you should go with the sugar cookies," I said.

"Can we buy some new cutters?" Kevin said, closing the drawer.

"Don't we have any?" Kent asked.

"All I found was a snowman and a tree," Kevin said.

"We'll get a new package at the store," I said, ruffling Kevin's hair.

I got a piece of paper and began to jot items from the recipe, talking as I did. "OK, now you all go wash up and put Karen's shoes on and make sure her face is clean. I have to make a quick phone call about the medical wives' meeting here tomorrow, and then we'll go."

The boys went through the dining room to the foyer. Kent paused while Kevin ran on up the stairway. "Tug, come on—we've got a lot to do."

Karen sat looking up at her me. She wasn't sure what was going on. "Can we get sickles?"

I came around and lifted her up from the booth and gave her a hug and put her down. "No popsicles today. We are going to make Christmas cookies!"

I turned my little imp toward the dining room and gave her a light pat on the behind. "Now, go on, and let your brother get you ready."

Karen took off to Kent's arms. "Better comb her hair too, and put on some clean socks," I added, aware that her little "Raggedy Ann" preferred rumpled hair and clothes. I had been so thrilled with my girl. Karen had gotten over thirty dresses when she was born; and I had once envisioned covering her in bows and satins like my friends did their girls.

Finally, we had gotten back from the grocery store. Karen stood in the kitchen by the stove, eating her popsicle that she had gotten. After all, I had to bribe her with a box, and a promise that she could have one when she got *home, if she would behave while the boys and I found the ingredients that we were so excited over.*

We I had set to work on making the cookies as soon as the grocery bags were emptied; and now, we were hovered around the table, with Kevin and I measuring and stirring things into the big bowl as Kent read the recipe. Karen sucked her popsicle and watched. We were having so much fun. Karen was probably thinking that it sure would be neat for her to get her hands in all of that gooey stuff in the bowl–then get to lick her fingers; but she was being quiet and staying out of the way.

Out of the corner of my eye, I noticed that Karen had finished her popsicle, then dropped the stick into the sink, and wiped her hands on her red corduroy pants. When she noticed the blue smears she had left, she darted down the hall–most likely to remove the pants and stuff them behind the door before I would notice.

When she came back into the kitchen, she was barefoot, and shirtless as well, but neither of us three looked up nor told her that it was too cold to be running around with no clothes on. Guess I figured there was time for that as soon as we got a batch of cookies in the oven.

I was dusting my hands from where I had made a large circle of flour in the middle of the table. "Kent, hold the bowl with both hands so Kevin can scrape it clean. Yeah, oh, nice. OK guys, now each of you take one end of the rolling pin and get the dough as round and smooth as you can."

The boys and I were completely absorbed in getting the dough just right. "Is it thin enough?" Kent asked.

A few minutes later, when the splat first hit the center of the dough, we three jerked back, at once holding the same startled expressions that quickly changed to horrified.

"Mom," Kevin said, his face twisted in disbelief, "she's peed on the Christmas cookies!"

We hadn't even noticed her climbing up onto the stool; and now, there she stood in her practiced position–with a smug smile beaming.

We three began to laugh, and Karen laughed with us; and the laughing became so infectious that none of us could bring it to a stop for about five minutes. I had tears rolling down my face; and Karen looked like she couldn't quite understand how her Mom could be having so much fun and crying at the same time.

Our laughter finally slowed down and then stopped. By this time, Karen had climbed onto a chair, where she continued to force the chortles and sniggers that her brothers had been making.

She looked up. The three of us sat staring at her. Karen was puzzled that we were no longer amused.

"Mom," Kent said, "aren't you going to punish her?"

"Punish her?"

"You can't let her get away with behavior like that. Now we can't make cookies!"

Kevin leaned toward Karen, and she slid down in her chair. "Yeah, you can't let her get away with that," he said.

I glanced around at the three of my children. The little one knitted her brows and pouted her lips. How could I have been so callous?

I stood and bent toward my daughter. Karen pulled back.

"It's all right, Sweetheart. You're not going to be punished."

"Not going to be punished? Mom!" Kent said.

"Punish her after we've just spent five minutes laughing at what she did?" I said. Kent crossed his arms.

Kevin came around the table. I had picked Karen up into my arms. Karen had buried her head in my shoulder.

Kevin looked up at his sister. "See what you did?"

"Kevin, have a seat, " I said. My voice was serious. I sat back down on the yellow leather, with Karen in my lap.

After a few seconds, I said, "I have done a terrible thing." The boys were surprised. I gave Karen another hug, and turned her around onto my knee.

"We left your little sister out of all of the fun–from the beginning–we didn't ask her to join in the planning, the buying or the making. And that was my fault. I should have known better."

Karen turned her head up toward me. She realized that she was not going to be in trouble, after all. I glanced over to Kent. He was still frowning.

"Well," he said, "how about what she did? Are you going to let her get by with it?"

"She was only trying to get our attention."

"Well, she sure did that!" Kevin said, laughing again.

"Here's what we are going to do:" I told them. "We are going to all clean up this mess–Karen included. Then, we are going to the store again; and Karen is to fully participate as we concoct a second batch of cookies, beginning with the groceries."

Friday July 18, 4:00 PM

The light is quiet on my lids. I stretch my shoulders comfortably under the spread before opening my eyes.

After grabbing a pillow and stuffing it behind my shoulders, I reach for the three-ring binder and pen on the table beside the bed to record my dream about Granny and Grampaw. This recent shaking in my hands makes it an effort to write.

Aunt Ethel told me that

when Grampaw got caught up in the spirit–what they called getting happy, nothing could hold him down.

I couldn't imagine it. The only Grampaw I knew was a stiff old guy that said a long and stodgy table blessing. Well–we all change. My children remember, but will my grandchildren be able to believe that their grandma once had roles in musicals and danced on the stage?

Right now, rolling over the Turkish carpets is a major effort. Kevin had to untangle the fringe of the rug from my wheel this morning. We were late for therapy. I AM really trying. Why can't I get happy? I'm so tired. Therapy takes all day: two hours getting ready, an hour's travel, and two hours at the rehab.

The canned roar of laughter bubbles up from the television downstairs. I glance around for my vehicle. It is gone. The door at the end of my hallway is closed.

"Karen!" The noise rises up the stairs. "Mother, Kevin!" Am I going to have to CRAWL to the commode?

I can't crawl up onto the commode.

"I need my wheelchair!" Karen's taken my independence! She is probably draped over it watching that goofy show. I squall out again.

No response.

I pick up a hefty book from the table and hurl it. As it thuds against the closet door and falls to the floor, I see it is my hard bound copy of *Leaves Of Grass*. Damn, sorry Walt.

I hear them burst through the door before I see them. I swipe my face with my palms as Karen stumbles in.

"Mom! I thought you were taking a nap," she says, wide-eyed.

"How can I get to the bathroom when you take my chair?" My voice squeaks like it's on glass.

Karen steps back and Kevin puts a hand on my shoulder. "Now Mom, just calm down, nobody's actually stolen anything," he says, with that twinkle in his eyes.

"This is no comedy!" I look up to Mother.

"Let us help you Judy," she says. She whips around to Karen. "Get your mother's chair!"

"Well, I was only borrowing!" Karen's gestures are exaggerated, her hand on her hip.

"Now, Tugger," Kevin starts, "Nobody's–."

"You two are going to have to do better in helping to take care of your mother," Mother interjects with a tone of authority.

"Granny, I'd say I'm doing a lot. I stay up half the night working in some hell-pizza job, and then I get her to therapy–."

"Now I won't have cussing around me!" Mother snaps.

"What's the big deal?" Karen yells.

"Hey, what's going on here?"

Well–Vedi has joined the jolly family hour.

Collapsing sideways onto my pillow, my legs are hanging awkwardly over the side of the bed .

I clutch the mattress to keep from spilling.

After Vedi wheels me from the bathroom, he helps me back onto the bed.

He tilts his head and grins. "Can I join you, my Irish redhead?"

I extend my hand. "You must be exhausted too," I whisper.

He scoots beside me.

The rest have scuttled off to *Wendy's* for their dinner. They will bring us back something. The air is cleared, there have been apologies and hugs all around.

"At least the squabble seemed like old times," I say, leaning my head onto his chest.

He begins massaging my thigh.

I nuzzle into his chest. The smell of his skin is so naturally sweet. The mosquitoes always want to suck on him. We lie close without speaking.

Then, he halfway sits. "Sweetheart, I had lunch today with the head nurse on a new physical therapy wing they have recently opened at the Rehab."

"Oh yeah?"

He studies me seriously. "They only have eight beds at present. Eventually, there will be forty. There is an empty bed."

"I'm already doing therapy."

"You could go in as a resident of the floor, stay as long as six weeks, get therapy all day long with the other eight. It's called a community."

"Can they help me?" I ask anxiously. "Would they accept me?"

You skim along silver rails that out-race rivers, slice across hardtop and gravel roads, jump off below the coal temple in Logan, West Virginia. Go further back into those jutted hills and shadowed valleys than solid wheels can turn. The musky darkness of the evening has moved in around the gray frame houses, all the same, in a row. You bump along the one-lane rutted course toward the shine and commotion by the river.

The white wooden church seems to be held aloft in feathery hands. In the light of the sooty fog, music streams from open windows, which widen as you sweep forward. You are carried in, along with a fistful of lightning bugs. The critters circle and signal above the folk gathered up out of the fields and the devilish cold mines for a Wednesday night prayer meeting.

Gladys' older sisters, Ethel Emmaline and Lura Ella, are there on the front pew, just the way Ethel told it years later.

The church is reeling, clapping a steady beat, straining against the bars, singing, "I'll fly away, fly away, oh, glory, I'll fly away. When this trial on earth is over, I'll fly away . . ."

And there's Grampaw Perry himself, Alonzo Leonard, son of Nepolean French Perry, and grandson of Richard Perry, immigrant from Ireland, fugitive from the potato famine.

Lon is lithe, got happy and full of redemption again. He's dancing on the backs of pews. His slicked red mane flops an unsteady beat against his forehead. His black plowing boots are polished to where the deep creases turn up glad, the toes like dull headlights, going every which way at once. He's leaping, sure as a tightrope walker, feeling the power, filled with the spirit, ready to go, needing to be higher than the floor, tripping like a vaudeville showman down on one knotty pine back and skipping up to the next, light as a dandelion fluff, nodding to his fourteen year old girl.

Black-haired Ethel holds her hand across her eyes. Her younger sister, Lou, looks a lot like eight year-old Gladys. Lou has buried her red head and freckled nose in Ethel's side.

Nobody else's father dances on the pews. In the aisles, maybe. Not the pews, across every last one of the pews and back. But neither breathes a word of complaint to their parents; or even looks back with rolling eyes at brother, Augrey Alfred, or sister, Myrtle Hespert. No one can question, that tonight, Dad is filled with the spirit.

He, who doesn't believe in folks doing the jitterbug or waltz, is dancing like King David before the ark.

Gracie Bailey Perry, Lon's wife, sits at the back, wrapped in the singing that warms her soul, swinging a hobnailed shoe, puffing her corncob pipe. Soon, in time, to be known as Granny, she transforms into a genie on top of the smoke. It turns and lifts her as it slides through the bell tower. The bell peals and harmonizes with the assembly's sounds. All ascends from the dank clouds toward the stars, glowing cinders, and you, too, get caught up, away into another light.

7

Merely A Door

Monday, July 28th, 10:00 AM

A metallic ping. Number 3 lights up. The elevator opens,.

It is, after all, only a door.

"This is it," Vedi announces, shoving me, in my wheelchair, through the opening. As we enter the hall, the battling noise of drill hammers overwhelm everything else. I feel like an immigrant. Maybe it's merely a door but

Once you pass through, who are you?

"Are you OK, Mom?" Karen has bent down to my ear. I nod, yes. As I glance around me, Karen looms green and tall over my shoulder, and Kevin is melting into the wall, his blue eyes sparkling in a frame of beige, his arms folded over a T-shirt that reads, *We All Live Downstream.* Vedi grips the handles behind me. I can feel his weight through the steel and leather. I think he must be fidgety, already counting who has he to see in the main hospital as soon as he deposits me here.

Vedi is shouting over the blast of machine-gun air. "Margie's the supervisor. This new wing is her responsibility!"

Like a white beach towel, she floats toward me. Red polished nails compress into two crabs swooning over my hands, which are white-knuckled, roped hard and tight. She is laughing.

"Not really," she answers, "there's a web of specialists–physical, social, occupational therapists . . ."

Her touch is warm oil, her words are water, she is a professional. Because of my tremor, I want to release my hands. I flash a smile at her spreading lips, red in front of my face. I start spurting words, remind-ing myself to take it easy, slow down, I'm not on trial. This is not an interview, it's only another door.

"Vedi told me, so glad to be here, glad to be starting, coming, be learning how to manage . . ."

Shift your tone of your voice, I tell myself, use the mode of the guest.

"Manage," I repeat sweetly, yes this tone is better, "LEARN how to live in this vehicle on my own."

Take a breath. "Oh my, what a bright–what a sunny place!"

We are in a glare of sunlight jarring through the window. I twist around and squint, turning my head over my shoulder to gaze out the window that spreads ceiling to floor. Beyond the glass, black and red figures look like they're dancing in air.

"That space they're finishing out there–that room will one day be our community room. They're tearing up a concrete ceiling to make a floor."

A bundle of voice and scuffle, we advance down the hall. It is a tunnel of fluorescence and polish. Comes my muffled thought: You should have waited a week.

One door of the tunnel opens. Purple toes protrude, then a whole splinted leg propped on a metal ledge, then a man in Bermuda shorts wheeling his chair. His toes zigzag like the prow of a boat. His hands are gears turning the wheels. He guns it off in the other direction.

"Matt was hit by a dump truck," Margie says. Her voice jumps in my headache like piano notes.

I tap the tips of my fingers on the cool metal. I'm here. OK.

The Crystal Ballroom of Hotel Roanoke glittered and tinkled with the dresses and china and voices of row on row of tables of women; and I sat at the head table above them, unable to focus on my lunch or the person talking to my right and left, because as soon as dessert was over, I would have to sing; and I was just getting over a cold and wasn't sure about the high notes; and I had strained my throat a bit by yelling at the kids because they would not get ready on time—so that I could get myself together after Kent left for school and I dropped Kevin off at kindergarten; and I hadn't yet decided what I should wear, and I really had not found time for that extra practice that I needed; but, I breezed into the hotel as if I didn't have a care and spoke with my hosts in a voice full of confidence, for luck would be on my side.

I had practiced almost enough and had shown up on time, almost; but, there were just so many things to do in a day's time that sometimes I just wished I didn't have to be an artist.

When the time came for me to sing, after all, I was able to lightly grasp the podium, and no one could see how much my knees shook all through the song.

After the meeting, I graciously replied, "Oh, go on, you could!" when a woman said, "I would give anything to be as relaxed as you."

We pull into the nurses' station. There's a small welcoming committee. A buxom Practical Nurse named Clara, says, "Shall we give them the fifty-cent tour?" She moves behind me. I feel her take over my chair. My *entourage* follows.

Through the Occupational Therapy door, we float by conglomerations of tables with metals, wooden rings, blocks, and utensils, exercise mats on pedestals, and weights and bars.

An elderly man sitting at a table seems to be using an afflicted hand. The therapist sits next to him. "That's it, Ralph, you're getting it." His hand holds a wooden block. It wavers, palsied, suspended over a square hole. He struggles, jiggling over the puzzle, unable to control the fit.

I feel like an intruder.

He glances sideways, aware of us. He snarls, "To hell with it!" and drops the tool. The block bounces from the wooden table to the tile with a hollow clack and two clicks.

The therapist stretches. "Hi there! I'm Dolly." Her mop of black ringlets encase her warm face.

In Physical Therapy, Margie says, "Here comes Annabell, your physical therapist, with your new roommate, Ruth." A scuffing and plunk wearied chain-ball-kick rhythm moves across the room. I note first, the four white tennis shoes on the tile, then the frame of a big-boned blonde holding the arm of a woman in brown pants and blouse bent into her task: To lift the walker, plant the walker, then step-slog-step. She looks to be over sixty, her hair white and cut close to the scalp.

We go to the small dining room where a rectangular table takes up most of the space. "Now," Margie says, "this is where you will come for three meals a day."

"You bring Judy each meal?" Vedi asks.

Margie laughs. "No indeed. She must get here on her own. Patients wheel, walk, limp, or hobble in here to dine."

Vedi gives me that cockeyed look.

Kevin steps over and pats me on the back. "You can manage that, Mom."

I try to imagine six patients with wheelchairs and crutches getting up to this table. Where does Matt protrude his toe? They've got to be kidding.

Out the door, we follow Margie around the broad hallway. It circles the therapy and nursing rooms like a race track. Patients' rooms skirt the rim. Stainless steel rails at waist level run the entire length of both sides.

My room is down from the nurses' station. It's as large as three private rooms, a pale yellow. Ruth is resting on her bed, in the opposite end from mine. She is still in her gym clothes. The two beds have windows, with rows of drawers built into the wall between. We share a toilet. A wide-door shower is at the center, and two lavatories in a long counter align the wall to the right of the door.

"Clara will help you get settled," Margie says. "I'll be back in after your family leaves."

"Shall I help you unpack, Mom?" Karen asks as she picks up my bag.

"Oh, no, she'll do that herself," Clara says, intercepting the bag. "That way, she'll know where to find them."

From the looks of things, Ruth has been here for a while. The sill of her window is crammed with drying yellow and red mums, a spider plant, magazines, a mirror, oils, and make-up laid on a tray in the middle. Plastic balloons, tied to the foot of her bed, assertively bob, *Get Well Soon!* There must be fifty cards taped onto the wall beside her drawers. She catches me staring.

"You can tell how long a person has been here by the amount of cards on the wall," she says demurely. "See that drawing? Sent by my little ones in Sunday School," she whispers, lowering her eyes.

Tuesday, July 29, 4:45 PM

Ruth could be laid-out in her coffin. Her eyes are closed in the peace of the pill they give her this time of day, hands folded onto her chest and wrapped in a warm glob of wax that's supposed to ease the joints. If Ruth's hands don't improve, she will soon not be able to grasp. The sunlight shears through the slits where she's closed the blinds, splaying a bridge of light above her. Through my open shade, the sky, buildings, and trees are dismembered.

It's quiet on the floor, the therapists gone. We rest before dinner—that center-ringed circus: Matt eats sideways, wedged at a corner of the table. Ralph's right hand is strapped to an elastic harness. I have no appetite. My hands tremble and I'm nauseous, especially at the table; but food is energy. I force what I am able, taking little bites washed down with water. Across from Ralph, I try not to watch him in his efforts. He wrestles with the air, trying to guide his special soup spoon to his mouth. Its handle, made fat with surgical tape, helps. He dribbles and slops more food onto his bib than he manages to get between his lips, but the nurses refrain from assisting unless necessary. He's sullen, cussing and groaning. The social therapist says we are family now.

In two loaded cars, we hit the highway's black dust, your Ana–grand-mother, nieces, nephew, aunts, you, me, your daddy, and the youngest dark-eyed cousin, Edip, who took to sitting on your lap all the way to Ates's summer place in Turkey, on the eastern shore, in a town named Tirkirdag.

Over the mountains, through a rainbow of vehicles—jam, horns, and oversized tires droned around us. Wind swiped the sweat off our cheeks; and for a day and half, we were a clan. Off down an August dirt road, we bumped and found a porch, a beat-up wooden rocker, benches, trees that cried for trim, and a yard settled into heat and wanting our noise.

The table on the porch had seen its share of meals and songs. They swapped old family myths you and I didn't know.

We found fat melons in the village, bought a whole trunkload, sweet and round like dark greet tits. The sisters sat and snapped beans while your Ana ate grapes from the arbor in the back, your older cousin, Bilgen, pro-testing, "They're too wild and sour," while old and wise Ana grinned, a look of mild delight to have them all for herself, her eyes soft and moist, so full of all of us.

Ates was soon in trunks. "Come on down to the beach, Karen!" he yelled, "Come while they cook."

I, already five pounds fatter than I had been a week ago, pulled into suit like you, who were coaxing your daddy into his.

Small boats hugged the shore where we splattered in. The Marmara Sea was shallow there, but cold enough to make us numb; and you said it felt as if your blood had all gone to your head to find the only warmth left under your skin. We were dizzy being together and knowing we were bearing the cold for each other's sake. We went out chest deep. Ates's son, Edip, kept jumping off your shoulders. We dived through legs and splashed till all we felt was warmth.

We later dragged the charcoal out, scraped the grill, had village bread, beans with olive oil, kofte, cucumbers, tomatoes–so much food that the table yawned, grew hands and arms.

Stuffed as eggplants, we walked the beach at sundown, watched the boats bob in the distance: gold nuggets blinking on and off.

Sated and with salt sticky in our hair, we filed back, arm in arm, then sang and danced old Ana into early morning bed.

We slept in quiet common sweat.

So far, there have been only five of our family members at the table, the sixth one not yet out of his room. Clyde's room is two doors down from here. I am overwhelmed that he also has GBS. All the way up to his ears. They tell me that he had cardiac arrest twice. The doctors inserted a needle into his heart to get it going. Twice. He was on a respirator for several weeks. Still can't use his arms.

Today, on the mat, Annabell massaged every muscle and joint in my body. She worked hard, as if she could rub the newness back into my limbs. It's her job and she's good at it. Dolly's started me lifting weights to build up strength in my arms and hands. She says I should be positive and elated that only half of me is numb. But the news about Clyde hangs over me like the January sky you keep looking out into, expecting sleet. Can I survive, knowing what I now know, if paralysis starts creeping up again? What if I begin to get straightened up only to face it all over?

We never sat around the kitchen table all together because Mamma worked; and on Sundays when she was home and would cook the big meal, we would eat in the dining room.

I ate cereal on cold foggy mornings before school at the kitchen table. Crunching cornflakes, Jon, at the end, slurped to irritate me. The table was plain and white and sat back against the window. It had hard wooden chairs.

I'd stack the dirty dishes up on it, Sundays, because it was my duty to tidy up after we ate; and often we had company, and they always assumed I liked my job.

"I wish my daughter would clean like yours," they'd say to Mamma;

and Mamma'd never brag or take a compliment for me. It was too much like taking one for herself. But, I hated to see that table stacked full of Mamma's dried-on chicken gravy. It was hard as glue to scrub off the pan that she'd never take the time to soak; and I couldn't go out to walk in the woods with Rosie until after church, after dinner, and after I did up the dishes.

Sometimes, Daddy said, he wouldn't be able to sleep for thinking; and he would get up and sit there at that table and smoke and stare into the deep silence.

9 PM

"Oh, I keep it for when visitors come," Ruth says, running a comb across her head. Her dangling feet slide down the side of her bed to the floor. She scoots her fuzzy slippers, her hand balancing on the night stand, and deposits the comb on the window ledge.

I focus on the Styrofoam head sitting on the counter by Ruth's sink. The dumb, white face is a flawless female in tranquillity. The champagne-brown Pekinese wig on top of that head is about as apt as topping a birthday cake with broom straw.

"Is it hot?"

Ruth turns, swinging her left hand out to catch onto the bed. "Thing makes me look like a hussy," she says in a snappy tone.

"I see."

"No you don't." Her tightened eyes look to be searing a hole through the air to me. "Wouldn't fool nobody, like a raccoon on my head."

I hadn't meant to open a can of worms. She put it on last night when her nephew came to visit, told me he bought it for her. I recall a strand of their discussion: "Then, what are we going to do with you?" The nephew had asked her that.

Ruth and I are in this boat together, I'm thinking. Better get used to the bounce of the waves.

"It'll grow back," I say. "Pretty natural color now." I smile at her until her eyes soften, and she scoots back up onto the side of the bed.

"I was getting better," she says, pouting, "before I broke a hip."

Shaking my head, I'm wondering at the depth of this poor widow's miseries. The nephew's concern seemed financial. A nursing home has got to be a question.

"I was able to care for myself real well for a while. Then, out of the blue one day, there I was in the kitchen frying bacon and it looked like my legs just plain gave out right from underneath me and down I went. Just luck the pan with all that hot grease was still on the stove."

Multiple Sclerosis.

I get a picture of her struggling on a kitchen floor, in pain. Yet, if she had her wits, her first thought had to be how to drag herself up to turn off the fire under the grease. I know too well the dilemma of dealing with your heavy body on the floor.

Dr. Miller was almost certain that I don't have MS.

"Did it take long to diagnose your condition?"

"Why, it took a good five years before they finally figured it out."

Ruth stares at me for a few seconds. I return her gaze without answering.

11:00 PM

I'm bleeding. I forgot to pack anything for this, lost track of the days. This warm, oozing out of me is exciting, a reminder that I'm still functioning even if I can't feel it. All these days, my ovary has been struggling for life as normal.

Had been fiddling my way across the Greenbrier, was low you know, August, infested with fuzzy stones just covered with what you might call encampments of razor-thin snails. Was casting in deep-shaded holes, fisting my toes around these rubber thongs I had got to protect my feet.

Well, then, out of the blue, it hit, leaped, streaming oily colors through the haze–just like them wild rainbows are named for. I jerked, slipped, had my leg in a hole clear up to my knee. Sneaky current stoled one of them thongs right off of my foot. Should've knowed.

Then I lunged, lost the grip of the rod, thinking, Can't let 'er get away!

Plunged toward the reel, came up with a twisted mess of line around the rod, that fish knowing the advantage of its stream, mind you–and me, hauling hand over hand, sidestepping toward the bank ever time I got the edge, it just a zigzagging to throw the barb, me, trying to anchor with the protected foot.

There was my blasted thumb, sliced by the plastic line, blood drops smattering in the froth around my feet. Had the pole jammed up under my arm while I kept sorta teetering toward the bank. But, I tell ya, I had snagged it good.

Worked it finally to the shallows, nine inches of whipped rainbow! I could hear the celebration pounding in my ears.

Caught it up between my knees, unscrewed the hook, grinning how me and my prize were both bleeding like stuck rams into that dazzled pool.

But–I stepped backwards, scraped my naked foot over a whole bed of them snails. Guess we both leaped at the same time.

Dang thing waved its fins, turned its head and winked right at me before it split back into the water.

Wednesday, July 30, 9:30 AM

Diagonally, I cross the path Ruth's chair has made on her way out the door to Occupational Therapy, OT, parallel park at the sink, then reach for my toothbrush and paste. Always, I am in a queasy state, but now food doesn't taste right–the eggs metallic, the toast cardboard. Swallowing a gag, I open the tube.

A housekeeper enters, pushing a large dust mop.

"Well, hi there!"

I turn, foam seeping from my lips, raise my eyelids in reply, return to my task. Craning my chin, I barely spit over the rim of the sink.

"They tell me you're taking a little trip this morning," Nadine says, bending to rustle dust balls from the edge of the wall.

"Tests and x-rays," I answer, catching a faucet with my left hand. I haul myself forward and bring water to rinse my mouth in a cupped right hand. "Sending an ambulance to cart me over to the main hospital." I add, swiping my mouth with the towel.

"You want me to let you know when they get here?"

"Sure," I say, swinging my chair around. Nadine begins pushing the broom again as I wheel toward the bed.

"This new wing is different. I used to be at the main hospital," she calls from Ruth's side of the room.

"Oh yeah?" My covers are knotted in a heap. I was so stiff and sore this morning that it took longer to get myself out. The hospital bed is too high for me to back off onto the chair; so, I lower one end of the bed and transfer out of and into it. So far, I haven't missed breakfast. I begin to straighten the cover and sheets while Nadine glances uncomfortably at me over her broom..

"You-all on this floor are mighty brave," she says, coming up behind me to watch. "Can I be personal?"

"Yes," I respond, wheeling toward the end of the bed to smooth the blanket.

"How'd ya manage to dress, I mean, since you can't—you know?"

"By lying and sitting in bed. My Blue Barges are hardest to put on, maybe outside of my pants," I tell her, fluffing my pillow. I picture myself, on my back, finessing my pants up over my hips.

"Blue barges?"

Spinning back to face her, I point to my tennis shoes.

"Yeah—all of you wear them up here."

"Tennis shoes are a requirement for physical therapy; but, my feet are so swollen that my husband had to get me the men's size—wider, you know. You should see me contorting on the bed to get into these shoes—like stuffing a turkey."

Nadine's nodding with an open-mouth expression as if I'd just explained Einstein's theory.

I chuckle self-consciously. "Roll around and wiggle a lot and no sweat to it."

And no need to talk about frustration and pain. When Dr. Godwin's partner, Dr. William's, made rounds at breakfast, he asked if I had any complaints; and I said, "Not a one."

"Well, best of luck with your future," Nadine says, turning on her broom and pushing what she's gathered up out of the door.

Our Ana's hands, smooth as potatoes, turn the demitasse cup. Her lentil eyes dredge the cup. There's messages in the coffee's mud. She holds the handle by two fingers, flipping this well of questions and answers like a butterfly's wing. Past and future also appear on the porcelain rim and wall. She reads it upside down; and raises her half-moon brows at a clutter in the hollow. Does she see black olives, onion slivers, folded carpets that might look all lost and wasted, heavy as ice? At the bottom–does she sees a ring–a vacant chair? Ana crosses her hands on her breast for a prayer. The sting of lemon blossoms filters the air. "This fal all good, all good. Sure," She is a bit too insistent. "even snakes and swords–they mean good fal–what's you say–fate?"

Thursday, July 31, 10:25 AM

"All right!" Annabell shouts. My butt gratefully sinks back down onto the padded board. My whole torso starts to crumble into the solid security beneath me.

"Na–straighten up." Annabell catches me by both arms. My blood is throbbing as she supports me until I pull my spine upright and steady my breathing. When she releases her grip, my eyes latch onto hers. My palms slide out to balance this sitting, as we have practiced.

"Get yourself stable, you're wavering," warns Cliff, Annabell's young assistant. This position of no support for my back is difficult to maintain for more than a couple of minutes. A heavy crook begins to knot between my shoulder blades.

After a moment, the two sit at my sides, each with a hand on my back before we attempt the more daring trick.

"How did getting up feel to you this time?"

Yesterday afternoon, the two of them pulled me upright and onto my legs. My fear was that my ankles would break.

"It feels so TALL."

Her blue eyes crinkle at the edges. I watch a halo the light makes around the blonde hair of this woman I've come to clutch as if she's my savior.

"Every time you work with me we do something more." She is teacher, Amazon woman, my hope.

"That's right," she answers. "You're going to come up onto your feet again. Cliff, get the table, please."

From the center of the floor, Cliff brings one of those hospital bed trays on wheels. What the heck? He cranks it as high as it will go, then steps over to my side.

"This time," Annabell says, "When we have you up, I will count to three. The table, you reach for and grab on the count of three, because we are going to let go of you."

As she looks at me, I am sure she must have seen the jab of alarm that just struck through my head to my stomach.

I scoot to the edge of the padded table, using hands to adjust legs so that feet are apart. I study my shoes, wishing they were even wider. My therapists grasp me above the elbows.

"Steady, steady," Annabell says quietly, "let your knees stay bent."

I feel like I am hang-gliding.

"OK, on the count of three, we are going to let go!" Cliff yells. I tighten against the breath I've been holding.

"One–" Annabell shouts.

Sizing up the table, I note it to be a little below the height of my shoulders.

"Two–"

"Ready," Annabell whispers.

"Now–three!" she yells.

My arms cast out like ropes and latch around the edges of the table. They clock me to hanging on for a full fifteen seconds.

Back down on the mat, Annabell is a coach on the sidelines of a championship game. "Last two times you were putting most of your energy into your fear of falling. This time you won't do that, because this time, your muscles will be saying, 'Oh yes, we remember how to do that,' and you will put energy into helping those muscles do what they were meant to do."

I look at her warily.

"You know," she goads me, "STAND!"

This third time, lunging upwards, grabbing the table, I am a spectacle hanging out of some remote, high window, clinging to a ledge, knowing that if I lose my grip and courage, I will be forever falling.

I glide on rivers I've known: the Ohio, wide, algae-green and snuggling deep along the thigh of Huntington; snaky Mud River, where Daddy used to fish, overgrown, forested; and Twelve Pole river, that they call a creek. I roamed its banks with Jon and Pete.

We three teeter on the top of a concrete wall in mud-laced shoes, a piece of cardboard stuck inside our soles because of the holes. We had to see it—our river grown wild and high as a Georgia pine, like Mamma told.

The railroad's wall supports the bridge that spans the gully, now filled with the roiling Twelve Pole Creek. We stand transfixed as it whorls past and floodwaters lash against the side of the bridge. We brace against wind. It's rank—like rotten straw.

Clutching the shoulder of little Pete, I lean and tip toward the flood. The four-year old holds his own ground, his thin legs stiffening against the torrent. We've seen The Lone Ranger face such things.

I almost lose balance on my clever feet, so skilled with banks, but Jon yanks me back by the hem of my dress. He's eleven, responsible, and in for it bad if one of us drowns, or even gets hurt. Our biggest fears are the tanned fannies we'll surely get if Daddy finds out we've snuck down here.

But, this is somewhere we HAVE to be. We've come like outlaws to see for ourselves how ole Twelve Pole has been bewitched. Wild horses couldn't hold us back. We could hear its roar from back up at the house.

The demon's mouth is foaming-red from the just-plowed clay it has slurped from fields. It's streaked with black ribbons, where Jon says it gorged at hillsides of coal. The monster belly is full of leaves; and headless trees with twisted arms reach up to grab us, as if they could. We count two handfuls of swarming wet wings, five broken bottles, a go-rounding tire with its frayed rope waving, a washing machine like Mamma's on the porch, and a single blue boot.

We dance on the edge of what's swelled up. Is our Creek at the bottom? Our swimming pool? Our island of weeds and rocks, where we've carved-out towns, and dug winding roads for matchbox cars? We built houses with indoor toilets for our match stick people in the coarse, wet sand.

Above the rumble of the flood, we yell, High-ho! and hurl silver bullets picked up from the tracks. Our trains rumble over the creek, caboose with balcony, trainmen with smiles and bluestriped caps, day and night, on sched-ule, always, and we call and salute them clear out of sight.

This trestle, this canyon, this ransacked green bank has seen us swing like careless, skinned apes who let go the vine without any fear, to streak like stars into the hole, the cool, tan waters of Twelve Pole Creek.

Little do we guess, how, this very night, the hungry mouth will grow wider yet, and the throat will huff and puff to swallow the bridge. It will creep up the gravel, tongue onto our grass, slobbering its way right into our house, the small white house we'll have to abandon, along with the wood stove, the ice box, the back porch, the dandelion yard with the banty rooster, the mason jars of berry jam, the purple chicks we got for Easter.

We cannot fathom how it will be–to leave home behind, where the well and outhouse will tremble together in a coppered tide that will churn them askilt, or how, later, our home will sag, the stinking ruin dried-on by the winds when the tired and lamenting waters recede.

We believe in wonder. On the faith in our feet, our souls fly high. We do not even guess at the awful deep. We are held above harm by invisible wings.

Friday, August 1, 6 PM

I'm sitting by the elevator looking out the picture window at the end of the corridor. The workmen have gone home. Their jackhammers finally ceased two days ago. I'll be long gone from here by the time they are able to move patients into the room they're building out there.

Through the wooden framework they've erected, I look onto Jefferson Street and watch the cars. Where are they all going? My path stops right here.

I put a hand to my chest and finger the crystals. I can feel no power emitting from them. Running my fingers along the defined edges of their bullet shapes, I wonder if being hauled up onto my feet by Annabell and Cliff is truly progress. My left leg aches more than the rest of my body. I must remember that Dr. Nolan has repeatedly told me that pain indicates healing.

I wonder about my life as a path that has brought me to this glass barrier. I think of the past year. I picture that day in April when I rushed from teaching to the office. I parked the little red Spectrum I was driving on an incline in the lot, opened the door, put my leg out, and turned to get my bag. The wind slammed the door against my ankle. Vedi examined it. There was no broken bone, but it was so badly bruised that there was an indentation where the door hit me. I didn't stay off my foot that day, even though the ankle hurt. Just like I didn't stay home in bed when I got the flu in April. Took Tylenol, vitamins, and liquids and didn't miss a beat, controlled the fever. Took a month to get over it. Got it again in May. Treated it the same. What was I trying to prove? Kept telling myself, Next year I am going to find some way to reflect on my inner self.

Whoa!

I jerk from my reverie when I hear the ding, and wheel around as the elevator doors open.

When he sees me, his mouth is wide in greeting. Kent, in blue jeans and a turquoise T-shirt with a white *Grateful Dead* skeleton doing a dance on it.

"Hey," he laughs, "How did you know I was coming, Granny call? I told them I wanted to surprise you!"

"I didn't, she didn't, and I am!" I extend my arms.

"Got a night off so I could run over the mountain to check up on you," he says, laying a book in my lap. When he raises up, I look at the book.

When Everything You Always Wanted Is Not Enough by Rabbi Kushner. "Thought you might need some reading,. It's a best-seller."

"Very timely," I tell him, thinking it not strange at all that my thoughts have brought this book and my son to this window.

A bit later

Kent and I linger in the therapy room. I have just given him a graphic description of my adventures in here. ". . . like skateboarding off a mountain!"

He is elated. "You're going to do it, Mom, in no time!" He cheers, moving restlessly around the room, fingering the equipment. "You are the one that told me that we have to open to the power, Mom."

He stops and stoops in front of me. "Believe," he says emphatically, looking me in the eyes.

I run my hand across his temple and down the side of his hair, pulled back into a pony tail with a leather tie.

"I know," I say, "but now, sometimes I wonder what I've been trying to prove with my life."

"Why do you think you have to prove anything?" he answers, standing up. "Look, let me remind you that you're also the one who has a sign tacked up in her office that says, *No woman is required to build the world by destroying herself.*"

I never knew he noticed that sign. "A 19th century somebody named Rabbi Sofer. I use it teaching women's classes sometimes."

"Time to use it on yourself, Mom."

"Well, I am trying to tackle coming to grips with this handicap–using the Twelve-Step Program I learned so well."

"You're talking about when you decided to stop drinking?"

"Got to the place I couldn't tolerate it. Person needs a program to deal with what they don't understand. Best way in the world to handle it."

"Well, one thing you know is–it works."

"The greatest help I ever knew in my life was allowing my spirit to merge once in a while with the Great Spirit. But, I've been thinking that I let myself get run down this past year, trying to take on too much, as if I'm indispensable–let my immune system get weak–opened a door for this virus to sneak in. I'd think by now I'd have learned better."

"Dad was telling me last night that the older we get, the more we know what we don't know. Looks like you needed time to reflect on yourself and you got it."

"Son, did you ever hear that old Turkish tale that asks, How does Allah make a poor man happy?"

Kent laughs. "No, but you're going to tell me. How?"

"By making him lose his only donkey." I poise my head and wait.

"Wait a minute! OK, I'll bite. How?"

"By then—letting him find it."

I don't give a second thought to tying the room deodorant up under the lavatory. But, by August, my baby is on the move–explorer of the decade. Kitchen cabinets and drawers on floor level have to be wired together. Our few valuable curios are put up. my days are devoted to running after Kent.

A danger is forgotten, tucked quiet as a wasp's nest under the bathroom sink. And it is only a matter of time. Kent is destined to discover the door left open where he will crawl on muted knees and palms to pull up where the curious smell hangs waiting.

I hear the sudden silence of the apartment and quickly seek him out, room to room. But I am not quick enough. When I lift my son, he plants a fish kiss on my nose; and I smell the musty hint of decomposed pine. It's on his hands, too. I stoop to find a quarter-sized jade colored bauble hanging from its string. How could I have overlooked this?

Out of the room to the phone, holding him side-saddle on my hip, I rush while he giggles, thinking we are playing horsy. I reach the poison control center. They tell me the deodorant contains DDT. We must hurry. My heart is in my throat, the child is bouncing astride my hip, squealing with delight. Must change his diaper. No, no time for diapers, no time to take him to the children's' hospital.

I phone Vedi. After long moments, I get him. He will meet me across the street. No time to fix a bottle. My cursed memory could kill my boy!

My thin legs tread the air, feet sure of where they must go with my wriggling nine month-old bundle. I check his breathing on the way down in the elevator, eleven floors. Please, God, don't let it jam again. He spews healthy gurgles and cheeps. Still time.

When we bat through the double doors of the Roswell Park Cancer Center, I am hit by bright blue and florescent everywhere. A nurse in leather shoes with a pencil wants to take history but I tell her there is no time. Her eyes are puffy. I am explaining when Vedi and another doctor come up. I watch the nurse's white shoes as we whisk down the hall. My calves are quick to catch up with my child's urgent scream. He rejects her strange arms.

I have become a guilty on-looker. My son, strapped down, can't understand. His cries and gagging cough rip through my ears. I tiptoe to the opening between Vedi and the other doctor and the nurse. Kent's chest is sucking at the tube.

The doctor jerks out the tube. Kent's eyes are round and pink with fright. He thrashes for air. My baby can't breathe. His pink cheeks have gone icy blue.

The tile beneath my feet sinks from under me. My head expands. I am a bag of sawdust with a hole, fast sifting away. Two men and a woman in white bend over my baby, while I lose substance. I wail, "You're killing my son!"

Helpless. All I can do.

Vedi pivots, works his mouth: ". . . her . . . get her . . . out."

The room reverberates.

A large hand yanks me from the room.

There was no deodorant in his stomach; but for two weeks my child gagged and coughed, his throat raw with infection from the tube. I followed him everywhere he went.

Five years later, Kevin found a bottle of chlorine bleach that my Mother had left within his reach: A similar scenario with similar outcome.

My babies put their noses in poison but some divine hand kept it out of their systems. There are no answers to some questions.

8

Gypsy and Shiva

Saturday, August 2, 10 AM

An amorphous silhouette, like a dark Shiva, eclipses the morning sun, shadowing me, slouched in my wheelchair here in my room. A Shiva, who destroys yet restores, snakes multiple, silicate arms through the blinds.

The shadowed fingers slip around the plucky, black-faced Shasta daisies singing their lullabies from Vedi, reminding me that he has not forgotten my favorite flower. The Shiva-fingers trip across the cover of the book that our friend, Rahmat, brought in to me, his telling me how lovely it is to study a novel formed almost to perfection once upon a time. The shady fingertips smooth against the baby blue Bermuda shorts in my lap, the cloth folded back against the wide elastic band, easy for pulling them over and off of my hips, a present from Mother, who sends practical caring, singe the edges of the cards on my wall, growing daily like a garden, posies from Aunt Lou and Pauline, my friends Rosemary, Ann, Velma, and brother, Jon, tokens caught with me in my moment's rapture with light that seems to emphasize how my present is a symbiotic mixture of release and gain.

I exhale, slowly. The shadow moves on.

Part of me is glad to have a day off, no need to push past the headache, the peppered eyes, all of the muscles caught in a rock-hard aching I will not speak of, will instead, focus on the power of positive thoughts and speech which produce endorphin, hope and harmony nurturing my ills, will not allow negative into my space, will fix on finding ways that work, forget the pains, side step the fears.

Nurse Sarah breaks into my reverie with a scuffle and lilt. "It's a beautiful sunny day outside, Judy!"

With a sweep around, I meet the happy face of this nurse who works the week-end shift. She striking in her white pants, shirt, and a cap with insignia.

"I've gotten permission from Dr. Nolan to take you on an outing," she states diplomatically, waiting for my reaction. I clutch my palsied hands in an attempt to contain my alarm. Sarah's eyes flash from my hands to my face.

"Just downstairs, outside on the patio," she continues, stroking her words as if she is trying to convince a first-grader to get on the school bus.

Why should I want to go outside? My thoughts are racing. "I can enjoy the sun right here," I say.

Sarah steps closer and lowers her voice. "I know, but I really need your help. Sam would like to have a smoke. He can do that on the patio; and furthermore," she says, with an air of conspiracy, "Ralph's spirits would be lifted ever so much by a bit of fresh air under the leaves."

I like Sam. His wit creates a warm energy. I picture him as I watched from the door of my room yesterday afternoon, Annabell's left arm across his chest and hooked into his right armpit, her right arm supporting his hips by hoisting him at his back by a belt, his left arm wounded by the stroke, but his right hand grappling at the steel rail that lines the hallway. "You're doing fine!" Annabell said. She coached him as they humped along. From his gasping, and from the sweat pearling down the side of his face, I could see that Sam was in great pain. I bit my lip and swore by such courage, that, if I can only manage to get on my feet, I will attempt to make an effort half as noble as his.

"Wouldn't you like to get Ralph in a good mood?" Sarah asks.

I haven't yet seen Ralph exhibiting so much as a fair mood. Ralph was probably angry with the world long before he had a stroke; yet, for some reason, I want him to like me, and that's so silly. Certainly, I don't need the approval of grouchy old Ralph. But I would like to see Sam get a small reward.

"Who's going to be out there?" I ask. I'm thinking of hospital staff, doctors, acquaintances. A lot of friends don't even know I'm sick, this being vacation season.

Sarah straddles my footrest and grips the arms of my chair with both hands. "We're only going to stay a half hour," she says firmly. "It'll do you good, but don't just think of yourself. We are a family here, and we support each other."

Ralph and I, sitting diagonally like two wedges of a pie, stare through the glass panels of the nurses' station watching for Sarah to return with Sam. Two aides will have to be called to assist in getting the three of us down to the patio. From the corner of my eye, I note Ralph's turning toward me and staring hard. It doesn't feel like a friendly move.

"This Wierdo trip your idea, yes?" he growls after several seconds. I look at him, shaggy-headed and unshaven, a King Lear without a horse, still looking for a fight, the testosterone in his blood nowhere to go but to his mouth.

"Why would it be my idea, Ralph?" I reply, attempting to make it sound more like a statement than a question.

"You're the one," he rails, his eyes fixed on the floor, "always trying to act like we're suppose to be playing games in here, like some damned Pollyanna, like some shit-assed nut that doesn't have sense enough to know we're all too sick to go lollygagging out in the cold."

I correct him. "It's hot out, and I didn't feel like going either, Ralph." My voice is hoarse. "And now," I mumble to myself, "I wish I hadn't agreed to."

I'm trying to be an adult about this, trying to understand where he's coming from. I hate this throbbing thickness in my throat. How can I hold onto this morning's resolution to be positive?

"Cold as a goat's turd," he says, sullenly.

We've been down here on the back patio about five minutes. So far, no one has even noticed us. I'm parked so that I don't have to look at Ralph. The patches of sunshine skip and change as the breeze rustles the leaves overhead. The shifting pattern dances on Sam and Sarah. They sit relaxed, both patient and nurse, filling the fresh air with smoke. I've enjoyed an occasional cigarette, but nicotine stimulates me. With my system wired like its on some kind of speed, the thought of taking a drag gives me a shudder.

"Judy's a writer, scribbles all the time," Sam remarks after blowing a smoke ring. We watch it lift and widen out of shape.

Sarah leans toward me. "What do you write, Judy?" I laugh. "Poems,–stories. This spring, my partner, Rebekah, and I were working on a writing text for students and teachers."

"How interesting," Sarah says, "but there's probably not a whole lot to write about around here."

"I'm getting sick and tired of your mouth running," Ralph says, pointing to me.

Sarah is reprimanding Ralph. Sam is telling me to ignore Ralph. My eyes are changing to water which will be all over my cheeks when I bat my lids.

Ralph's a sick old fool, I tell myself. He's not my father, he's not important. Looking away, I watch the sunlight bleed into the leaves.

3:30 PM

Rebekah's bantering startles me. "You almost died. How can you lie calmly reading a book with such a title?" I close *Chronicle of a Death Foretold* and lay it on my table.

"Marquez," I say, leaning back on my pillow, "riveting writer."

"Still keeping that journal every day?" she asks.

I nod. "Pure stream of consciousness." Our eyes converge at my mentioning one of the steps in our unfinished book of writing lessons.

"I gave a Hollinsummer instructor a copy of the "Gracie" lesson, and she tried it," Rebekah tells me, sitting on the foot of my bed. Widening my eyes, I mock surprise. I like that lesson because it's about Granny. I get a thrill to see students get inspiration from Gracie's character. I think about Ralph when I remember the lines where Gracie says,

Now, nobody's all ugly, though some are pert-neer. Look again and find somethin' somewhere on ever body God's made that's near-well nice.

"Really," Rebekah continues, "and I was told it went rather well, so part of you WAS at Hollinsummer, after all."

I know that my friend is trying to compensate my sense of loss. But I've not only been away from my activities, I've been disconnected. How can I explain Purgatory to one who's in the middle of being so many things to so many people all at once? I look out the window and sigh.

Rebekah tears open the package she's been fiddling with and offers me a treat. I take it. "There's one board I wish we weren't on," she says seriously.

"Which?" I ask, tonguing the mint.

"Blue Ridge Writers Conference," she answers, "the one which is apparently now not going to happen." The candy grinds between her molars. I inhale deeply, sucking in the potent smell, my sinuses opening.

"What do you mean?" I ask, blinking.

"The keynote speaker engaged for this October can't come. The board members have scattered for summer vacations, and appear to be thinking to let the conference ride until next year."

"But, there are good writers to be gotten right around here," I say, pushing the pillow up behind me so my lower back won't throb.

Rebekah slumps forward onto her feet, retorting, "And who's going to get them? Can't do it on my own, got Keith to think of." Rebekah's Keith is only six months old. She's described how he is learning to crawl.

Rebekah watches me manage my carcass by scooting until I have my legs hanging over the side of the bed.

"Look," I surmise breathlessly, "I know we can get a keynote by making some telephone calls. Then, we'll contact *Writers In Virginia* and ask for a grant."

"We?" Rebekah says, hesitatingly sizing me up as I sit wobbling slightly.

"My brain is not in my feet," I whisper, guessing her thoughts. "I can use the telephone," I add, mimicking sarcasm. "I can talk, Lord knows."

"Here we go again," she says with a knowing quip. "Take heart, World," she adds, raising her voice and shaking her head of long, thick curls, "a hospitalized cripple and a mother with more than she can do already are at the scene!"

I crunch the last of the thin, sweet circle with my canines, relishing the sensation in my mouth. I'm savoring the excitement which only a creative challenge can bring about. Lord, I have missed this feeling!

"Oh rats! We're WOMEN!" I shout, raising one fist while clutching the mattress to steady myself with the other. Rebekah takes a stride toward me and grabs my fist, then lifts my other hand.

"WOMEN!" she calls.

There's energy in my veins. "We both have ideas already," I whisper, leaning into her dancing eyes.

Rebekah turns again at the door before going home, where she'll make calls, between diapers, to board members who may be in town. I grin back at her.

"I'm glad you didn't die," she says, her voice crooning.

"Get out of here, I've got phone work to do," I say, flapping a hand toward her.

Rebekah projects a sage look at me before replying. "You don't have to do this, you know."

"Oh—don't I?" She presses her lips tight and nods in understanding.

Ever since she was a kid, her favorite guise had been Gypsy. She had played the Salvation Army sergeant, Sarah Brown in Guys and Dolls, and

Polly Peachum in The Beggar's Opera; but the fun roles were Brigadoon's Meg Brockie, and fortuneteller at carnivals. Fortune telling was just a matter of watching the little movements of the client's eyes, a sudden a jerk of the hand or an increase in breathing as various subjects were mentioned; and the rest was being open to the muse.

As planned, when the evening of Rebekah's Halloween party got under way, Vedi phoned Rebekah's house. She answered in the kitchen so that the gang would hear her replies to Vedi's explanation of why Judy and he were not at the party.

"Judy just today found out she's pregnant? Great!"

"Oh, depressed and sick in bed is she? We'll miss her."

"Is she going to be all right?"

"Well, in that case, do you think you could get away for a little while and come on alone–since she's sleeping–or do you need to be with her?"

"That sounds good. Then, come on. And tell Judy I'll call her tomorrow."

A half hour later, Vedi stopped to let Judy out of his car at the foot of the long drive up the bend to Rebekah and Neal's house. Vedi looked at his wife. Sometimes she was like his fourth child. He loved it. She was sticking her hand in each of her breasts to make sure the sanitary pads were amply reinforcing under the low cut blouse. Her chest and neck had several coats of dark makeup base, the same as her face.

"There's so much black mascara on your lashes. What will you do if it gets in your eyes?" he said.

She threw him a sultry glance. "Are you kidding? They're even hard to bat."

Her cheeks were deep rose and her lids were violet. "Be careful not to lick your lips. You'll eat off your sexy mouth," he said.

Judy opened the door and gathered her Turkish peasant skirt and shawl with long fringe. Her suede boots crunched the gravel. "That's the least on my mind," she said, as she closed the door.

She turned on the flashlight, and he drove slowly on up.

Judy stood in the dark, pulling the scarf from Bursa tighter under her chin so that the dark wig, which protruded from it, would not be too obvious. She shook her head to hear the jangles of the tiers of silver hearts on her earlobes. She was glad to get a chance to wear them. These had not fit in very many occasions since the Seventies. She held the flashlight in one hand and her tambourine in the other. The gobs of rings and her painted nails flashed the full moonlight.

As she approached the flickering forms–scattered around the blazing fire in the barrel and in the yard, she began to hit the tambourine and sing a made-up song in a made-up language. She was intending to affect an accent that sounded something like a Sicilian raised in Transylvania.

She spotted Dan, sitting on a large log with his girlfriend. If she could fool him, she was home free. She ambled nearer, singing in a voice that she projected low and gravely. When she passed in front of Dan, she paused and stopped singing, and looked him over head to toe. He glanced at his girl-friend and down at his tennis shoes. Everyone was watching, and Dan didn't like the spotlight to be on him. Judy smacked the tambourine hard once, then bent her face close to his.

"Vel," she said, trying to look like she could just eat him right up, "vat uh hahn-zoom brute you are!"

"Excuse me? I'm an English professor. Hi."

The Gypsy ran her finger down the side of Dan's face and stopped it under his chin. She stared him in the eyes. "You, I know. Professor maybe, but rrrooman-tic, ooh." She pursed her lips.

"Nope. Uh, this is my fiancee. "Fraid we don't believe in fortune tell-ing." Dan presented a tight smile and pulled back. Judy knew she could certainly read his mind at that moment. He really wanted her to go away. But, he did not recognize her.

Rebekah came out. "Listen up everybody," she called, laying her hand on Judy's back. As they came closer, Judy could tell that Rebekah was pleased with the Gypsy.

"We have with us here tonight the famous Madame Moonstar from Boones Mill."

Judy dipped her head to her sides and front, to acknowledge the honor of being who she was. The fire in the barrel crackled and sent up a spray of stars.

"Probably some of you have heard of her, or better yet, been to her."

Judy raised her arms as if to receive or bless them.

"*Madame Moonstar will be telling fortunes in the living room to all who wish to explore the future.*"

During the next two hours, Judy had not a minute to pause for a drink or even a potato chip. They actually lined up and stood waiting. The Gypsy sat amid the flicker of candles and incense. They came to her one at a time, sat by her on the couch, and held out their palms. They were taking this seriously.

"Oh, you have big struggle ahead. Is hard, for you have secret sadness in heart not much people know."

"Yes, yes, I do," the man whispered, "but will it ever get better? Will it hold me back?"

"Always like secret island in big river; yes, it will be. You will ride river to new places, yes; but island always yours."

"Here, I want you to have this," the man said, slipping two dollars into her hand. Judy slipped it in her bosom, then thanked him profusely. So far, she had made fifteen dollars in tips, which she didn't know what to do about. Naturally, Rebekah and Neal weren't paying her. This was a party joke. But the guests were not catching on. Judy knew some of them; and she could tell they believed that she was Madame Moonstar.

"You are the first person to really see into my soul," the young woman said. "Can I come to you on a regular basis?"

"Is much to ask. I have ailment."

"Can I at least have your business card? You don't know what this has meant to me."

"I no here to make more customer. Already too much. Make tired."

The woman looked disappointed and stood waiting to hear something else. There was still a line outside the door. "OK, I have Labekah derange appointment. Yes?"

After two hours of this, Judy was beginning to get anxious. They were taking her for real, at least for a fake real. If Rebekah came in, as planned, and told them it was all part of the masquerade, and then, announced who the fortuneteller really was, it could get very uncomfortable. Most of these people had asked the Gypsy some very personal questions about their lives.

When Rebekah called everyone into the kitchen for the awarding of the costume prizes, Judy told Vedi to exit with her out the back door. Rebekah *didn't know where she and Vedi had disappeared at first. Then, she saw the car was gone. Rebekah didn't tell until the next day; and then, she only told a few.*

August 5, Tuesday, 10:15 AM

The sound of metal chinking on metal draws my attention across the room in Out-patient Therapy, where Annabell has brought me today. A young man, stripped to his gym shorts, alternates a pulley. He has a handsome body, the build of a football player; but the skin on his torso and legs is mottled, like melted plastic. He must have been in a terrible fire. He pulls the weights, bending with fierce determination.

I speaking to Rodney, the GBS patient that my first therapist, Ella, mentioned to me. He still comes to OP regularly. "Did you have the flu before you got Guillain-Barre?" I ask him,

"Well, yes, I had this intestinal thing that had gone on for three, four days, but didn't think it amounted to much, or was anything out of the ordinary,–but somehow it led to this," he states, staring down to his legs.

"There's that fellow, Clyde." Rodney says, looking off to the side, "He had a wart removed from his hand the week before he got GBS."

I turn my head and raise a hand to my fellow community member, Clyde, who's being pushed across the room on a gurney.

"A wart is caused by a virus, you see," Rodney adds. We watch Clyde taken toward double doors. Annabell follows him.

"Wonder what's in there?" I ask.

"Oh, that's a good place," Rodney says, "big hot tub, whirlpool. They're probably worried about atrophy setting up in Clyde's muscles."

"Hot water must be comforting," I say, "the jets massaging, whole body floating." We stare at the door, and I wonder how I could get a hot tub ordered for me. Certainly, the shower feels great every night, like hundreds of little fingers untying the aching knots. Delsie doesn't have to assist me anymore. I've got my system organized to the detail, from undressing to placing a warm, wet towel on the shower seat to stabilize my transfer from the wheelchair, to pajamas. My fear of falling still overshadows everything.

"Glad you two have met!" Ella calls. She strides up to us. I ask her if she knows about Clyde's having GBS.

"Sure, I hear they're ready to start his therapy," she answers. I feel a pang of guilt for thinking I have had it rough, considering what Clyde has faced, and will have to face in the weeks to come. Glancing across the room, I mentally place a healing green light around the burned youth.

I look at Rodney, who also was totally incapacitated.

A bit later

"That's it, wheel right in between the parallel bars," Annabell tells me. The steel rails loom like an open tunnel at shoulder height before me.

As she instructs, I lock my brakes and turn the footrests back against the sides. I have scooted my hips to the edge of the seat, and am double-checking my barges to make sure they are planted squarely on the floor.

When I raise my head, I'm startled to see myself in the mirror hung on the wall at the other end of the bars, a stranger, straining back at me for recognition. Annabell's golden curls are shining just above my head, her big blue eyes watching me.

"Today, you're going to stand without my help," she says.

I study us in the mirror. I look bloated and worn. To stand? For weeks now, I have been marveling how people lift and blithely flit away with the grace of butterflies, all their muscles and bones working in a silent harmony.

I take a deep breath, reach out and take hold of the bars.

"Lean forward to where your shoulders are extending exactly above the arches of your feet. When you're ready, pull, letting your weight fall into your legs and feet."

I pull, moving forward, but unable to lift the heaviness of me.

Again. My veins flood with adrenaline, my breath comes heavy.

"I will do it!" I say, pulling with the right hand and pushing the left against the chair. My torso bends out. My left hand flies up and catches the bar as my butt comes up.

"That's it!" she's saying, her voice pushing strength into me, "–as straight as you can, feel the weight go into your legs, don't lock those knees."

My shoulders rock back and forth. So this is how it was with prehistoric humans testing the upright stance.

"Concentrate on what you're doing!"

I am up.

By my own strength.

The mirror's capturing this, but I can't raise my head. It wants to float off into some lemonsultry sunset. I squeeze the bars to bring it back. Cold sweat pops out from under my arms, on my face, my neck, my hands. I grip harder to steady the rocking.

Annabell is at the left side of the bars. "Release your right hand," she calls.

My mind is racing. I can't do that.

"Don't think about it, just do it!"

My eyes stay glued onto my feet as if they might sneak out from under their load. What if my ankles crumble?

My right hand obeys her voice. I wobble, focusing on the barges.

"Good. Now, let go the left hand, you can do it, I won't let you fall, release–release!"

She might as well tell me jump from an airplane without a chute. But she will catch me.

Prying my fingers up one at time, stretching them out, I'm finally balancing my whole body on one bone in the palm of my hand. I try to even my breath, give air to my brain.

"Up, concentrate!" Her words are echoing all around me.

Centering toward a dot on the floor, nailing it into the wood with the pressure of my stare, I raise my left hand above the rail. I can grab it again if need be. My whole body is pulsing pain. But I WANT to feel. It is MY pain.

I am standing, balancing like I'm riding on a surfboard, arms shifting to counter the weaving, except that I can't get a control on this bulk of me, and my sight keeps going dark and light in a sensation of breaking apart.

"Bring your right hand forward—catch back onto the bar!"

"Pull with the right hand, bring forward the left foot."

Left foot forward?

My brain shoves the MOVE message to my left foot.

The foot can't hear.

My eyes dart like needles from my hand to my foot, from my hand to my foot. My insides are turning to soup, sloshing under my ribs.

Off goes my head, tumbling into an cloudy gray. I hear roaring where I'm crashing in the seconds just before Annabell saves my fall.

It was October, and my two year-old Kevin was raking me up in a mound of leaves, his hair, slick as an elf's hat, framing his face, shiny gold as the tree at the gate. He was my thistledown, tumbling through the house, rubber soled and sliding on the rag rug across the tile. He was light, chasing the cat into the bedroom, under the table, a bouncer who opened wide for spoonfuls of bran but slyly sucked only the banana slices. He was the energy in magic, released by lost wands, a featherweight boxer of shadow dust, a sneazer of butterflies to whom Kitty would come with rubber-tongued kisses when he sat very still.

He was an anchor, a gleam in my eye, an October sage, who hugged my leg tight with the two small hands in a pile of leaves, saying, "Love you, Mommie," and I looked down and felt that grip, and said, "Love you too," and he said, "You know, I just waited in heaven so long to be born to you," and I reached out and pulled up the essence of what this babe knew into my lungs and held it there as long as I could before it spiraled up with the leaves into air.

How we twirled together in the mound of colors, me, balancing us on tiptoes of grace and ease.

Toppled candles, ruffled rugs, cereal dry in the bowl, a cautious cat, a bright leaf, windswept all through an open door where the clock stands—still flutters in the stir of my step out the door.

3:30 PM

"You two look mighty snug," Margie says, cheerfully regarding me, propped on two pillows, covers pulled to my chest, clutching a little white bear.

"Karen sent Bear to me. We're cold," I answer.

Margie tells me she knows about my big day in therapy. Everything is shared on this floor.

"You got mail," she says, handing me an envelope.

"Any for me?" Ruth calls, inching her walker out of the bathroom.

"You got two." She goes to Ruth's bed and deposits them on it.

I open my card from Aunt Lou, Mother's sister who's been the one to tie the family into each another's lives. She is sorry she can't be with me. She has broken her arm, also taking therapy. "Work through the pain!" she says. Her kidney is acting up. Uncle Frank won't stay on his diet. "Pay special attention to the verse on the front of the card—has sustained me through many trials." I turn the cover over:

They that wait upon the Lord shall renew their strength; they shall mount up with wings as eagles; they shall run, and not be weary; and they shall walk, and not faint.

Isaiah 40:31

I feel a quickening in my abdomen.

"Interesting news?" Ruth calls to me. I nod.

"Ruth, what do you think it means to wait upon the Lord?" I hold the card up so she will understand this reference.

"My preacher says it means be patient."

I switch the words, Lord to Higher Power. Patience, I think, what I have little of.

"I'm going to begin every day from now on," I say, "by asking that I be given the left-over patience of people who have more than they need."

Standing today, I was forced to focus on every second of that moment with faith that could serve myself—and trust in Annabell. Faith had to be stronger than the fear of falling. It was like flying through a monsoon without radar.

Daddy and Uncle Jon were only eighteen months apart–stuck in the middle of a large family–mostly boys, with Aunt Grace the second born and Aunt Ruth the baby. Aunt Grace was the nearest thing to a saint that any of us ever knew. Her dad was police chief and her mom took sick; so it was up to her to cook, wash, and clean for all those boys, who seemed like they would never quit their rip-roaring and settle down in their own homes. She courted one man for years and years before she finally married and left home.

As I grew up, we would always gather at Aunt Grace's after we put the flowers on the graves on Decoration Day. Aunt Grace cooked up a mess for all of us. She never ate much and she was a quiet woman, but she shared two secrets with me:

She was not really all that sacrificing about never taking the breast or leg pieces of chicken. She took the wings because they are the sweetest and most tender parts.

And one day when I went up in her attic with her, I found a pair of red dancing shoes.

"Who did these belong to?" I asked.

"Why, they were mine," she answered.

Red shoes? Aunt Grace? I was one shocked teen-ager.

"I had dreams when I was young–but things happen. My Mother took diabetes and heart disease, you know." She stood in the haze of late sunlight through the blur of a small neglected window. The sparkles of dust we had rustled up hovered in the air like bees. "Didn't marry until it was too late to ever have any children of my own," she said. She held her elbows with her hands and looked around at the hat boxes, the quilt on the old rocker, a pile of seventy-eight records, a yellowed lampshade, and boxes, hats and flower vases and other junk.

"I sacrificed my life for my mother," she said. She looked me in the eye. "You know, I shouldn't have done that. You nieces and nephews are the closest I'll ever have to my own. Make your own life, Judy."

I never told anyone about what she said because they would not have believed me. The myth was that Aunt Grace would not have had her life any other way.

Well–I did, of course, tell one person–my cousin, Jeanne. It was natural that Jeanne and I would love each other to death, since she was Uncle Jon's daughter between two sons, same as me. I, too, was a little more than two years older than she.

From early on, Jeanne was a match to fire my imagination. Sometimes, after dinner on Decoration Day, I got to go home with her and stay a week. She was as near to a twin as could be, and we made a pledge one day in her green backyard by the cellar door to never stop telling one another stories. We swore on a brown spider that had spun a web above the door.

But, after she ran off and got married to the football hero of a little town near Saint Albans, where her daddy directed the church choir, and then she started having babies one after the other until she had five, we lost contact for a long time. But I knew how she was raising those kids, using her God-given voice, and how she had become a prima donna in a charismatic church movement, and how she traveled with that group all over the world, and how her marriage just hadn't amounted to much outside of those kids being born.

Mother and I went up in the Valley to her church one time to see this big production of The Sound of Music where she was Maria. She was full of light every time she came on the stage. God, she could have made it big in the world of entertainment if she had gone on to college like her parents wanted her to do. The Light family, after all, was known for being able to produce a song and dance routine at the drop of a hat–and any one of them could make up the lyrics and movements on the spot. I'll bet she was a most innovative and exciting mother for those five kids.

When I stayed with her those long-ago summers, we played paper dolls in her attic, some days, from dawn to dusk. There were no TV soap operas, but we spread out our dolls and made families that had the same kind of romance and tragedy that had to be worked out–and our endings were always good. Spiderweb stories.

Hid in the August attic heat, we would waltz those paper dolls on the dusty boards–our stiffedbacked beauties with their modelperfect mates, romancing in a world of gowns and furs, glamour bought so cheap, cut so even, fitting our imagination to a T. Jeanne was mostly mouth and smiling under golden hair in those days, while big black wasp furtively fashioned its paper nest snug on the ceiling of our private space. We believed the wasp would never leave her nest to sting us as long as we allowed her room. Oh, we did dress those dolls up.

But, we never took them out and down the steps into the swarming streets.

9

Answer Box

Thursday, August 7, 10:00 AM

"Where did you live when you first learned to crawl?" Annabell asks. She's scooted up a chair to face me, seated on the mat that covers a low therapy table.

"Crawl the first time?" I flatten out my hands, which are angled at my sides as props as I practice sitting without a chair. My blue barges, I have squared on the floor.

"You were probably six to eight months old. Well, today, you're going to learn to crawl again."

"That would have been on the farm."

A two-story wooden house with broad porch and swing, a rolling green front yard sloping at the sides of a knoll, an old fat oak, and dense trees beyond Daddy's woodpile chopping block up from the dirt road. Granny and Mother holding me down on the swing, forcing a tablespoon of caster oil into my mouth.

"Mother says I walked at nine months."

"Do you have an early memory involving walking?"

"The first thing that comes to mind is bees."

"Honey bees?"

"Got stung all over once."

Yellow jackets, mean and feisty, won't sting if you leave 'em alone. All at once, Jon lets out a war-whoop, and tears off like a Jack rabbit up the side of the yard toward the porch. We must have been making an awful racket. Past the door, frazzling things zooming right on through a hole in the screen, made from the nosing of those ole Ruff and Bucky hounds.

"Wow. Anyhow, you survived it."

Granny and her no-fooling-with-you broom shooing them back out the door. Mamma washing me in the metal tub, covering me in soda powder, rubbing off the ones that hang on till they drown.

"'Course, I can't say how much is memory and how much is family myth; but I hear-tell that I was covered with tiny scars."

"We're lucky if we get scars that go away."

Annabell stands. "Slide back and lie on your side with your knees bent."

I follow her directions, resting while she is talking. "Babies come to crawling out of a biological memory. There is a sequence; first, the sitting and balance, and then, one day, a roll and folding over onto the knees and hands."

Once my babies learned that mobility, they were off like little bull-dozers. I peer up sideways from the mat. "I'm learning to stand. Why do I have to go back to learning to crawl?"

"Balance. Endurance. Coordination. Judy, I wish I could take you to a nursery school for inspiration. You could watch little ones crawl."

I roll over. Annabell coaches me. "Using your arms, pull your hips up. Balance—don't worry about being unsteady—balance on your hands and knees."

Pulsating like an aching tooth from head to toes, I want to collapse. Every maneuver is a strain of body and will. Frustration starts in—like an electric tingling all over.

Wait . . . renew their strength . . .

"Now, just like a baby, you're first going to practice rocking, letting the weight shift as you do so."

I rock.

"The trick is to keep from toppling. Babies work hard; but normally, they are little balls of energy with nerve fibers in their limbs that have myelin sheaths."

. . . and not be weary . . . and not faint.

"Our bodies," Annabell continues, "are built so that we have a balanced, alternate swing to our movement. Bring the right hand forward, then pull the left knee forward."

Easily, I lift my right hand and place it several inches ahead.

"Now, left knee."

Where IS my left knee? A panic showers over me as I turn my head, searching for my knee.

Thud, I tumble, frustrated, embarrassed, confused.

"That was great. Rest a minute and we'll do it again."

The next time I'm up, I'm hauling forward inch by inch. First a beetle on its back. Now, a turtle. Rebekah's little Keith feels very close to me. A plane of glass-thin light slides at an angle from the window and feathers into me. Can Keith's spirit loan me energy?

"Energy," I say between breaths. In this spirit, I travel half a yard.

6:20 PM

"What ya reading?" Vedi calls, striding across my room. I turn the page down on the novel and lay the book beside me on the bed. "Stories about strong Celtic women. Betty B. brought it to me yesterday."

"Betty came?" he asks, dragging over a chair. I reach over to take his kiss. He also gives me a large paper bag folded down half way.

"Betty drops by once or twice a week," I say, poking into the bag to see if Mother sent clean underwear along with the socks and shirts. "Tell Mother I'm in desperate need of a new bra." I drop the bag to the floor.

Vedi reaches across me, stretching to pick up the peach on my windowsill. His abdomen moves on top of mine. Feels warm.

"Do you mind if I eat this?"

I shake my head. He's been in surgery most of the day. It lingers on him.

He ravages the fruit, sucking as he hungrily bites into it. A pearl of amber oozes from the corner of his lips onto his white shirt. He splits its fuzzy flesh, pops the seed out, and tosses it into the wastebasket.

"Rahmat brought that peach from the Farmers' Market," I tell him.

He's chomping with a full mouth. Earlier, what dinner I had, I forced down with sips of water. Still queasy, never hungry, getting snacks between meals, I am relieved to give away food. Vedi gags, then grabs a clump of tissues and wipes his hands and face.

"Do you want some cheese and crackers?"

"No, your mom will have dinner for me." He checks his watch then runs his hand across my forehead, brushing my hair back the way he likes it, and slides his finger down my cheek where it lingers under my chin. His gaze strokes my red puffy face and dry chapped lips. The air is titillated with peach.

Suddenly, he notices. "What happened to your curls?"

"Got my hair cut. Jim came here."

"I'm glad. I didn't like that permanent. I like you natural, Baby–the way you were born."

"Your big, awkward Baby learned to crawl today."

"I know," he answers, dropping back to his chair and picking up the TV remote control. "I check your chart every day. You're doing fine."

He clicks on the television.

"Wait," I say, reaching for the gadget in his hands, "I've got to tell you something." He claims the remote.

"OK, What? I'm listening." He's glancing from the TV hanging at the ceiling back to me, flipping channels until he lands the news.

Why does he do this? I've told him I never watch TV. It makes my head ache. He arranges his visits with me to coincide with the news. My face flushes. He catches my look and lowers the volume.

"I've been running all day, haven't even had time to read the newspaper," he says. When am I ever again going to get a little of his bedside manner?

"Remember—Margie wants my entire household at the conference tomorrow," I say loudly.

Vedi purses his lips. His eyes veer to the television. He is fixed briefly on it, then he turns back to me.

"I hope they can all manage to organize and get over here," he mumbles.

"I should hope so! It's for the family and the staff to discuss my progress."

"Kevin will have to see they get here. I'll be in the office."

Doctors wives understand that their husbands have SICK people to tend to. Doctors can be late, absent, and excused without apology. The blood throbs at my temples. We are talking about MY health here, not some stranger's. What's he going to do if I can't become able to assume at least some of the family responsibility again? Mother can't stay over forever.

He clicks off the TV and lays the gadget down, then reaches for my hand. I pull back.

"What have I done wrong?" he asks boyishly.

Is it possible he really does not understand?

"I told you about that conference yesterday," I whisper between drawn lips. "If you had an emergency tomorrow, I have no doubt you would find a way to leave the office and drive to it."

He lets out an audible sigh. "Of course I'll be here if I can, but you must know that I speak with your nurses, therapists, and doctors throughout the week. If I'm not here tomorrow, I wouldn't miss a thing."

He waits for me to answer.

I wipe my eyes again and rub my hand across the tail of my shirt.

I stare down at my hands. For a brief moment today, I moved in a bubble of light. He can't really share my situation. Neither even can Annabell.

"Brought all my stuff–hair dryer, oh, see you have one. Gee, a new adventure, coming to a hospital to cut hair. I've gone to theaters; but, Judy, this is weird–all those people in the hall."

"Jim, you're going to help me as much as any therapist. Last two weeks I've felt like a frump. You know how we women are about our hair; but it seemed petty, and then–you call and ask what you can do!"

"OK, let me get at it. Did you just wash it?"

"Sure. Give me a style that leaves nothing to comb. Oh,–Delsie, meet Jim. Delsie's my afternoon and evening nurse."

"Hey, Jim, nice to meet you. Where's your shop?"

"Over on Wasena. Don't usually make house calls. Has this girl been keeping you entertained up here?"

"You're excitement on the floor, Jim. I might just call and come by next week for a set. See ya. Behave now, Judy. Got to wheel Ruth back from the day room, if she's ready."

"Delsie likes everybody, Jim. She's a nurse's aide; but for my money, she knows as much about patients as the ones with degrees–that extra sense, knows those little important things."

"Like–well, how do you want it? Short, I know. Just trust me, all right? Just trust me."

"So, have you heard from your cousin, Rusty? I brought all three of her books when I came to Rehab. Can you believe it? I get out to California and call her because she is your cousin whom you haven't seen for years, but tell me to call because she is a writer too–and she is laid up with a broken leg and starts telling me how she is deep into spiritual healing and crystals and auras and sends me these book of hers–"

"I know. I was so surprised last week to see them."

"I mean–what kind of books do I now need? Is that the Great Force working or what? Books on healing, and they are based on the spiritual self

healing the emotional and the physical. Have to write her, but where do I start; I mean, two months ago, I call her and catch her up on her long-lost cousin and then GBS happens–and this here story takes a while to tell."

"Gosh, Judy, I'll bet it is a pain to explain to people. Like–what do you say–well, one morning I woke up paralyzed and they said it was a virus?"

"The thing is, there is not a short answer, like–if I had been in a car accident. No one has heard of GBS, and they keep asking questions; and I get so tired of explaining it. I have thought of cards–sending out announcements–Judy wishes to announce the following–TA TA, and then just fill in the information and tell them you will catch them up on the progress later."

"Here we are, Ruth. Jim, this is Ruth, Judy's roommate. She wanted to see what was going on in here."

"Please to meet you, Jim. Couldn't get my hair dresser to come in. Had to be taken over to the main hospital–and they won't always take you. You have to pay for it, too."

"Nice to meet you too, Ruth. Gee, all this attention makes me a little nervous. This won't take long, Judy."

"Hey, Mom, what's happening?"

"Kevin! I was going to surprise you with a new look. This is Jim. Jim– Kevin, my son."

"Brought you some chocolate chip cookies Karen and I baked this afternoon."

"You and Karen? Nice present. My being away is making you self-sufficient. Jim, want a cookie?"

"No thanks, and you are going to have to hold still. This place always like this? I'm going to make this quick and get out of your hair–so to speak."

"What's going on here–party?"

"Rahmat! Come in! Jim, meet our friend, Dr. Seif. Rahmat, this is Jim, the one I told you brought me in a cheeseburger last week and has come tonight to cut all this Little Orphan Annie off my head."

"Yeah, oh, all those curls in the sink, I see, back to your normal look. I just thought I'd stop by to bring you these peaches I bought at noon down at City Market."

"Rahmat works me into his rounds about every day–brings me books, goodies. Kevin, there's my telephone. Will you answer and take a message?"

"Nothing like this ever happened with my last roommate. We just watched TV, and sometimes the preacher would visit. Doctor, do you know anything about MS? They hope Judy doesn't have it, but I do. Took them five years to diagnose me. You just never know."

"Mom, it's Rebekah. Said Keith's crawling all over the place made her think of you—whatever that means. Said she's got some news about the conference, to call her tonight."

Friday, August 8, 3:20 PM

I wait in the dull haze the therapy room inherits once the afternoon sun has crept around the building. It's been five minutes since Annabell said, "Go ahead and transfer to the bicycle." She is hunched over her desk, preoccupied with weekly reports.

She takes a sip of coffee. "Hey, what are you waiting for? Peddle." There's a weary edge in her voice.

"To be strapped on."

She thoughtfully sets her cup on the desk.

"Strap on yourself. If you can, you'll be able to wheel down here and pedal this week-end while I'm gone."

Suddenly anxious as a kid given permission to cross the street alone, I stare at my feet.

Annabell turns back to her papers.

I sit, hesitating, but she doesn't look back.

I lean forward, press a shoulder onto the handlebar and hold for balance. I lower my arms, let my weight pivot on the bar until I roll my head to the center. Breathe, get the jitters out of the neck, go limp, don't topple. After stretching down, I reposition the left barge, tear the pedal's Velcro straps apart, fumble the shoe on with the left hand, and fit the Velcro back with the right.

Annabell appears totally engrossed in her files. Slowly, I churn my shoulders to ease the wrenching ache, then begin the move to lay the left shoulder onto the bar. The right foot should be easier to fix into place due to the left foot's stabilization. It is.

When I begin to pedal, Annabell scoops up her papers and leaves me with a wave and a congratulatory smile. She must have eyes in the top of her head. Pedaling's no problem once gravity becomes a companion to the motion.

This is my peddling time. Time has been suspended for me this summer with no distractions from my SELF.

Five minutes later, Annabell strides through the door over to the desk, where she tosses the files. She pauses, then crosses to the window and begins picking dead leaves from the potted plants. She speaks to me without turning around. I perceive her conscious attitude, designed to wean me from being so dependent on her. "Your imagination never stops, does it, Judy? I think you're lucky."

I grunt then sigh with a lilt.

She fills a pitcher and waters the plants one by one, giving some a little more than others. The daisies and mums need a lot, but the African violets take only what their saucers can hold. Their leaves must not get wet else they turn brown. This is Annabell's last task for the week.

When she puts the pitcher back, she stands, watching. Fatigue has slowed me.

She picks up a file and turns it so that I can see my name on it. She raises a brow at me, then opens the file and writes.

"I wrote that you are not to attempt standing while I am gone, with no one, not even your husband."

She picks up her jacket from the chair. I'm fixed on her leave-taking, a sadness swelling in my throat.

She returns my gaze. "Most patients, I have to encourage. You, I have to hold back," she says softly.

How attached to Annabell I have become, saddled in the emotions of a kindergartner whose mamma is going off for a holiday. I'm not alone, there are nurses, social therapists, family, and visitors who will come in.

But none of them can help me to stand alone.

You were the wings of my desire to touch–out the four blocks and down the gray gravel alley beside the railroad tracks where even no train ran anymore, my wheels spun in the black dirt–me, balancing bread, cornbread in a plastic bag, hot from the oven and my first batch; and Mamma was gone and brothers out on the streets, and no one there to see it when it came out of the oven and flopped out golden brown from the black iron skillet.

And then, I thought of you, Mrs. Shannon, my Baptist Young People's Union teacher, who lived with your hair pulled back into a bun in your tiny, clean house with your daughter; and I knew I could make it there and back before Daddy would get home if I hopped on my bike.

And so, I cut a big wedge, yellow wedge like sharp sunlight glancing off my handlebars and stuck it steaming in the bag. I took my bike out from behind the door in the outside hall where I kept it so nobody could steal it– there in our duplex–two story white house on Ninth Street West, my bike, red and white, and it could make the air move behind it like a cardinal's flight.

All the way over the red brick of the way straight out Ninth Street, I pictured your face at the door. How surprised you would be; and you would brag on it–no matter if it was any good; but most of all, you would know my love for you had wheeled me up to your gray frame porch there by the tracks.

You made me your assistant in BYPU every Sunday night, and I got to tell stories with the felt board figures, and lead songs too.

"You're a natural born teacher, Honey," you'd say. And always, with that smile.

I jumped off the bike and ran up the steps and knocked on the door. The screen door opened; and I held up my surprise.

"First cornbread? No–come Mary, see. And you only in the seventh grade, I can't believe your thinking of us!"

I couldn't stay, not even for tea this time, just had time for that smile; and off I wheeled again, my sprockets spouting and spitting. When I got home, they never even knew I'd gone.

6:30 PM

I look up from where I'm sitting on the side of my bed when I see the blue suit coming through the doorway. My neurologist hails me pleasantly.

"You're moving around a bit now," he says. There's encouragement in his voice.

"Each morning I'm so stiff I think I can't roll over."

"The best relief is to move. Work through the pain, but go slowly."

I wait.

He's jotting a note on my chart and stepping to the door to catch a nurse about contacting an ENT specialist to check my ear infection. I'll have to remember to ask him how his wife, Carolyn, is doing. She's always so willing to play for the Medical Wives Chorus whenever I need her–or maybe after twelve years it's time to give that up anyway.

"Now," Don continues, "for the good news." He pauses as my eyes widen. "I had a little talk with Doctor Miller. He has compared the results of my last test with his. The indications point most certainly to Guillain-Barre syndrome."

"You're sure I don't have MS?"

"Almost sure," he says hesitatingly. "For the time being, no more tests."

Hallelujah! I could almost start singing. "Be sure to tell Carolyn hello for me."

"She'll appreciate that. She's been a little under the weather recently."

"By the way, what's this I hear that Mary's in the hospital again regarding the cancer."

"I heard that too. Maybe you gals should have a phone visit."

"Right. I'll give her a ring. You know, Mary's one person, that when I think of her, I see her burst into that smile that can catch a whole room up in it."

"I know what you mean."

"Mary always represented, to me, the spirit of the medical chorus."

"Guess she's been in it a long time."

"Since nineteen seventy-three, when there were only twelve of us."

Truth is, I started the chorus out of my need to teach music.

"By seventy-six, when we sang for the state convention–then were invited to the national convention–we had forty-five members."

"Very positive, professional."

"Got a standing ovation and a check for forty-five thousand dollars to pay expenses for the bi-centennial program we designed. I wrote some of the adaptations and Betty Lesko made up some of the accompaniments. Each member had a special part in the program."

"Carolyn loved being in it. Well–have to finish rounds. Keep up the spirit and I'll see you Monday."

I bought a bra for that performance.

There we were, in our red and white checkered pinafores over white blouses, lining up backstage where we were being introduced to thousands of people. I wore the red bra and panties to match, in honor of the honor, thinking how spiffy it would be to stand before the elite audience of the nation's medical community, directing an elegant production in my secret scarlet underwear. But, I had forgotten that mine was the only back to the audience.

Nancy spotted the red strap beneath my blouse. "Judy! What do you have on beneath your blouse? My God, you have to get a white bra! And quick, they're introducing us now!"

"Thirty-four "B"–thirty-four "B"–who has a white bra that size, get it off, quick! Trade!"

No wonder they said we marched out with a gleam in our eyes. It was Mary's bra I wore. We all had on her smile.

10:50 PM

I pick up the phone on the second of its two short rings, knowing only Vedi can get through at night. My voice is muffled, but Ruth still turns over in her bed.

"Oh no," I answer, pushing up on an elbow. Vedi has just had a sixteen year old girl die on the table.

"I knew she was in bad shape before I raced out to the ER."

"Was it a car wreck?"

"Yeah–the Camero was twisted around a tree. Firemen had to cut the door off before the rescue squad could get to her."

"Sorry to be so far away from you."

Death comes like flicking off a light, and Vedi never gets used to life slipping through his hands, especially when it's a young person. I listen quietly, all I can do.

"I miss you," He whispers.

After we hang up, I'm wide-eyed in the dark. This life we take for granted is always on the edge of disaster.

Ruth pulls back from her bed the beige curtain. "Got to feeling like I was smothering," says, plumping her pillows.

In the jaundiced light, the bundle of Ruth's body looks like a miniature mountain range, the cavity between our beds, a gray void. Her knee moves under the cover.

"Sorry to have awakened you. Vedi's on trauma call."

"I figured that was him. What happened?"

"Did you notice the helicopter a couple of hours ago?"

"Can't say I did."

"Teenage girl lost control on Route 220 near Boone's Mill. Older sister gave her an ID card so she could get liquor."

I lie listening for a winding siren or the breathy whap-whapping of a helicopter–its red top glowing like coals in fog, beaming across the rim of Mill Mountain.

Bits and pieces of the nurses' voices bounce around in the hallway, slicing into our room along with shards of light through the cracked door.

I hope my kids are in bed.

Saturday, August 9, 2:50 PM

"So that's why the number's different," I tell her. Betty B. got a runaround on the phone line, trying to locate me. I hear a spoon scrape against a pan. She must be making supper before dashing off to her studio to chisel stone.

"So when did this happen?"

"This morning. When my roommate left for her two-days home-leave, they moved me."

I tell her about taking down and tacking back up my cards and putting clothes away.

"I would have trouble sharing space with a stranger," she says. I very well know how this willowy friend with her pixy haircut consciously guards the space where she creates.

It was refreshing to hear from Betty. I picture her, off to get in a few hours of work on the commissioned bust, then hitting the markets to load up so she can do the big family dinner tomorrow.

I remember her "Mothers" series last year, nine burlap figures, overstuffed with straw, assembled in an open field, ungainly, ungallant, of the earth, earth-colored.

The two of us flew up the highway to New York City with the giant "Mother" anchored to the top of the van with ropes. Late that night, in the exhibition hall, we jabbed the knife-sized needles, suturing the legs back to the hips from where the journey had torn them loose.

"Hey, Betty, what do you call me—a seamstress or a sculptor's apprentice?" Both of our hands bled into the burlap.

Bringing legs of stone or burlap to life means perseverance.

Later

"Ready for your snack?" Delsie says, crossing the room. It will be an apple, half a turkey sandwich, and some milk.

"Rain stop?" I ask, as she lays the cellophane-covered package on my table. "Yeah," she says enthusiastically, "but, you know that thunder and lightning?"

I recall the violent bolts challenging me through my window an hour ago.

"I was lying here by this window thinking how ironic it would be if

I got struck dead by a jagged finger of fate. Then, I remembered that public buildings are grounded."

Delsie flaps her hands onto her hips and gives a snort. "Can you believe this? Lightning hit Addison School about an hour ago. Just lucky the kids are on summer vacation."

A bit later

For about ten minutes, I'm reading, pleased to be getting past the middle of *Chronicle*. Then, slowly, I start to be aware of an eerie numbness creeping into my hips. As if I've been suddenly struck, I flinch, throwing aside the book. My hands are clammy. I look toward the door. Should I push my call button? I begin to massage my thighs and hips with hard squeezes. Oh my God, it's back! How can I go through this again? I'm shaking all over, reaching for the call button, holding it with both hands.

Wait a minute. I pinch my stomach. It feels OK. I hear Mother's voice.

Moving at least keeps the blood circulating, can't give up.

Carefully, I begin the transfer from bed to wheels, deciding to give it a bit of time. Don't panic, move, I tell myself, rolling out the door.

There's no one in the nurse's station, no patients in the halls. I am still quivering, but I'm breathing squarely down into my diaphragm. I'm going to overcome this.

Pushing my wheels hard, I sail around the wing until exhaustion overtakes the shaking.

"Hey you," Delsie calls, "What are you trying to prove?"

I grab my butt with both hands and squeeze. I can't be sure, but it seems better. I'm ashamed to tell her what a panic I had because my butt went to sleep.

Dumb butt.

"OK, just going down here to sit a while," I call back, gliding off toward the large window at the end of the hallway.

I park in a shower of sunlight, looking out to Jefferson Street. Tired and relieved, I begin to shrivel into my thoughts. Peaceful and quiet, I could be one of those old folks who sit on porch or market benches–watching time slip by, pondering on all the roads they've traveled. I cannot hurry to catch time. In this rare instance, there does not seem to be any need to be anywhere else, to do anything else except wait here, simply being in the moment, feeling as mellow as immersing in one of those warm springs we found in Turkey.

The tiredness evaporates. No wonder old people look content. I want to own this peace.

In psycho-drama group, Ann guided us on a mind-journey. We lay back in fat pillows on the floor in a darkened room with eyes closed. She made implications and my imagination took over a scene in this subconscious unfolding.

"The idea is that the inner self knows truth that the conscious mind chooses to lock away in order to deal with daily living," Ann had told us.

My subconscious had opened up a suggested room of my own invention, one set up just the way I wished it to be, a secret place, where no one else could enter, an attic garret in an old Victorian manor, secluded on a cliff overlooking a green sea that pounded huge rocks far below.

I entered from stairs that spiraled up and up, to end at a small weathered door that led into one round room with skylights in a vaulted dome. The other window was tall and narrow, opening to sky and sea. The colors of the room were browns and golds. Thick carpet and large pillows covered the floor and paneled walls, lined with filled bookcases; and there was a large desk built into one side. There was a computer, coffee maker, portable refrigerator, and Bunsen burner. There were candles placed about, and lots of papers and magazines.

Ann told us to explore and find a symbolic object somewhere in our space. I moved to where it was sitting alone on a table: a small green and blue handmade glass and lead box, the inside of which was mirrored. I took it into my hands.

Ann indicated that the object would contain a message from the subconscious to the conscious–that it would be the answer to a question.

Opening the lid, I looked at the reflection of my face caught in the box.

"How can I know self better?"

"In order to find self, you must lose self."

10

The Lazarus Club

Wednesday, August 13, 4:00 PM

"Can I disturb you?" he says, as he ambles toward me. I wheel around and hold out my arms.

"Sweetheart, what a nice surprise!"

Wrapping my arms around Vedi and hugging my head to his chest feels more comfortable than anything else in my life, like home.

After the long embrace, he drags a chair to my side and begins telling me about how he spent his day after surgery.

"I headed down to the park to sit for a while—you know, on the river, right out from the hospital." Wasena Park. Scout picnics, soccer games.

"Where did you park in the park?" Our eyes exchange twinkles.

"You know my special spot." Where he stops when he finds a break in his schedule or when he is on his way home. I picture him gliding his tires into ruts worn onto the grass, turning off the ignition, and lowering the right window to allow a cross-breeze.

"There was a grandfather down there on the bank teaching a little boy to fish. I watched how he held the hook while the little boy put bait on it." He pauses in thought, pressing his lips together. "I should have taken my kids fishing."

"Did your father take you fishing?"

"No, I never learned. Now, it's too late, the kids are grown . . ."

It's never too late for fishing," I whisper, laying a hand on his wrist.

The Greenbrier River with Daddy, my first rainbow trout, my line so tangled–but I kept balance until I reached the shore.

"So what is new today, Chief?" Vedi asks, changing to a lighter tone.

"I stood up with the walker this afternoon–what I was writing about when you came in."

"Take a step?"

"Couldn't make that lead in my feet move one inch."

He nods in commiseration. "Anything else?"

"The Rehab had a surprise picnic today."

Vedi seems to be excited that I've gotten outside the building.

"I learned something about being disabled. Some nurse came up to my Candy Striper and they had this conversation, using my wheelchair to lean on."

"Vedi looks puzzled. "What was so bad about that?"

"A disabled person's vehicle is an extension of their body! She propped her foot on my chair!"

Vedi places a hand on my knee. "She didn't insult you deliberately."

He always gets defensive about his profession.

"People block out the disabled because they fear a broken body could happen to them," I explain.

"Judy, this idea is stressed in nursing schools."

"Well, maybe that nurse missed a class! It was as if she thought I was deaf, dumb, and blind just because I'm paraplegic. It was so awkward."

"Dignity is an important thing," Vedi states.

"Talking up to people from a chair affects the psychological balance of the conversation."

"Thank God I had the good sense to get a chair when I came into this room."

Vedi stretches across his knees and grasps my hands in his. "You're doing so well, that I have a surprise for you."

"What?" I push my hands into his palms.

"I had to get permission from your staff here, but today I heard that I can take you out to dinner at the Sheraton Friday night."

He waits. My mouth opens dumbly.

"I've invited my three residents and their wives too."

I can't decide what I should say.

He watches me. I guess he is interpreting my silence as compliance. What is he thinking? Who are these residents and wives that I should want to spend an evening at the Sheraton in a wheelchair, in pain all over, feet on fire, eyes burning, hands shaking?

"I don't have any shoes I can wear with a dress."

"Shoes don't matter. You'll be an inspiration, they are doctors, they will see how brave—"

"Going out to eat isn't going to make me walk sooner."

I withdraw my hands. The very idea that he should be planning something like this without asking me. Does he think he can spring it on me, tell me it's arranged, and I'll have to go?

"Sweetheart," he says, in a controlled tone, "you need to begin to get back into the real world, socialize a bit. You need this dinner."

"Oh, especially since I've just gotten to where I don't want to throw up all the time. THESE days, I ONLY feel—all the time—like I've got a lifetime case of the flu!"

Vedi stands up and begins to haul his chair back to where it was. He's pulling away rather than discussing. He doesn't want to hear about how I feel.

"Wait just a dang minute!" I say, raising my voice.

He steps deliberately over to the door and shuts it.

"The real world? This ward is my real world right now. I've made an effort not to complain about my aches and pains—in order to live in the positive. I thought you would comprehend." Apparently, assuming that he will understand how I'm feeling is a mistake.

Vedi acts like a scolded dog. I don't want pity, but I deserve understanding.

"But how would you know, Doc? You're hardly ever Ill!"

I'm hardly ever ill! Was!

"If you were in my situation, do you think you would allow yourself to be hauled out with a bunch of strangers for two hours of added discomfort? I don't think so. You're the man who can hardly stand to take a shot."

Vedi walks toward the chair and slumps into it. I wheel head on up to him.

"Do you remember way back when we went to get the blood test for our marriage?"

He throws up his hands and lets them drop as he lets out a loud sigh.

"Well, I was determined to be nonchalant about the nurse's drawing my blood, to impress my doctor-fiancee. When it came YOUR turn, you would have thought that nurse was planning to cut off your arm!"

"OK, I don't like shots."

"You CRINGED, told that nurse she was being too rough. Whenever you get pain, you just generally turn into pale rubber." I look him right in the face.

"Judy, I thought you were more humble." His smile is saccharin. His tone is calm. "You shouldn't be so proud."

Would that I had the ability to rise and fling myself around the room.

Vedi gets up, eases across the footrest of my chair, and walks to my sink. He stares into it as if some message is going to bubble up out of the drain. An oracle maybe? I am so frustrated; but if I start to cry, and one of the nurses comes in, then I have to have this long conversation about why I am crying.

He comes back and politely bends to give me a peck on my hot cheek. "I will talk with you when you are in a better mood."

Seconds later, he's out the door. It closes behind him. A cold breath slips in and curls around my bare legs.

That was an underhanded, middle-eastern maneuver, I tell myself, staring at the invisible trail of him.

You lock the wheelchair, inch to the edge of the seat, spread feet to supportive space, your back to where shoulders parallel arches when butt is mid-air, test feet to be sure you can feel when weight is applied. Place hands on seat and push at equal pressure, pulling butt while quadriceps focus like fists; and you steadily come to where you balance on tips of fingers. You are almost straight but not locked, balance by the arm of the chair on one finger, check to see if your feet, calves, knees, thighs, hips, back, shoulders are all in balance, overlook any pain, remember to breathe deeply and evenly to give air to the brain. You have been nailing a dot into the floor with the pressure of your focused stare–let go of the crutch–that is, the last finger comes up–then LIFT, continue to ignore tremble, tremble of adjusting muscles, balance like on your first skateboard–arms shifting, lifting, and flying in reflex–a fluttering puppet–STAY up. But your head floats off into that lavender lemonsultry sunset. Cheeks drain cool. Time to swing back, grab cold metal, release, let weight go back, grab cold metal, release, let weight go back, deep into blue vinyl. You are hea–vy.

8:30 PM

A pecking at my door distracts me from my book. The knob twists, the door cracks. The shape of a big, pink fishhook jars through the opening.

"What?" I call.

A plastic flamingo bobs, pointing it's black beak in my direction. My mouth opens in anticipation of a spirited visitor.

The door fans back.

"Surprise!" Kevin's eyes are full of light and amusement. His face absorbs the delight in my face and sends it back to me.

"Brought you your state bird."

He wobbles the bird across the room, holding it by a metal stick in its abdomen.

"Don't let my mother hear you say that, you'll get her feathers ruffled."

He presents the treasure. "Oh, she already flew off the handle when I said it."

I hold the flamingo in both hands. "You can't say it's one of a kind."

"Talk about sticking your neck out," he laughs.

I place my hand on his. "I love it. Never thought I'd have one of my very own."

"Well, I know you're proud to come from a state that fends off winter and blues with pink plastic."

I throw him a "whatever" with my hand.

"So what's with you?" I ask, as I watch him use surgical tape to secure the bird's metal leg to the head of my bed.

"Oh, gave up the great pizza gig. Got to get ready for first year in college. Hanging out most nights at the Iroquois Club, no money for much else."

We study each other. My good buddy is leaving. No need to reiterate how I wish to be helping him prepare.

"Is Hampshire College ready for the Turkish invasion?"

His expression changes to one of mild concern.

"Mom, tell Dad not to open my mail."

I'm surprised. Our family respects privacy.

"What happened?"

Kevin begins to answer first with his hands, palms up, flouncing the air to emphasize his exasperation.

"I come home and Dad's reading the paper. `Did you see your mail?' he asks; then, tells me what's in it—my room assignment from Hampshire! I should be telling Dad what my room assignment is, instead of his knowing first."

"Did your father say why he opened your mail?"

"Yeah, he said he saw it was from the college and thought they wanted more money."

I smile.

"He has to come up with the money, for sure. He always has your best interest in mind. So tell me about your room."

Kevin grins impishly.

"I'm in a coed dorm."

Shaking my head with mock disapproval, I say, "Couldn't have happened in the stone-age when I was at Marshall."

"Mom, nothing happened then. You guys probably thought flamingoes brought babies."

"No, it was the storks, same as today."

"Joint bathrooms for the girls and boys. Hampshire is progressive."

"Just make sure you don't progress too far."

My son raises his brows and tilts his head.

"Now Mom, just what could you do about it if I did?"

I regard the statement for a moment, concluding that he is right. He will leave us and never really come home again, just like Kent. My chest sags with a sad weight.

"I really do wish I could be out running around with you. Helping you get ready." He sits down on the side of the bed.

"Speaking of getting out, what's this about the Sheraton?"

"Did he mention that to you?"

"He's pretty pissed-off that you won't go."

"It's not just that I feel lousy. It serves no purpose. If going to the Sheraton would help me to take a step, you can rest assured I'd want to go twice a week."

"Now, Mom, Dad always has the best in mind for us."

I smile back at his half-grin.

"Maybe you should be more straightforward and honest with him about what your needs are," says the sage.

Some kind of trendy social event in the Crystal Ballroom at the Hotel Roanoke, and they had gotten home earlier than usual. Vedi had gone to take Karen's sitter home.

Fourteen year-old Kevin was sitting at the table when she tripped into the kitchen from the foyer in her long emerald green gown with the plunging neckline and spaghetti straps. She needed a glass of water. She'd had a few drinks at the reception, and her eyes were glistening as green as her gown.

"Kevin!" she had said when she saw him sitting there. Her tone was as urgent as if she were about to tell him that Martians had just landed on the front lawn. "You'll never guess what I did tonight!"

"Now, Mom, did you topple the punch bowl?"

"You know how your dad leaves me at a party 'cause he likes to look over the crowd and talk to a few people he's interested in, and how I just jump right in and talk to whomever–"

"Is there a point to this?"

"That I got stuck with this circle of people I didn't even know."

"No problem for you in that? What else?"

"What else? The conversation was boring–eyesight–they were talking about how this one was nearsighted and that one was farsighted, and how and why contacts did or did not work; and I just stood there with my glass of white wine poised in my hand, and started to figure how I could grace-fully move on. The place was crowded, right? So, somebody had to be having a more lively conversation."

Kevin leaned back and ran his hand through thick hair that fell just below his ears.

"And?"

Vedi came in through the kitchen door.

"Hey man! What you doing up?"

"Well, it IS Saturday night. Watched a film with Robby and came on home."

"Sure. I'm going to have some cereal and bananas. Want a bowl, son?"

"Vedi–I'm telling him what happened tonight!"

"Oh."

Vedi crossed the kitchen and started down the hall to the bedroom. He called back over his shoulder.

"Be back, going to change,"

She sat down in the booth beside her son and grinned. He grinned back. "Whatever this awful thing was you did, you are enjoying it a lot, Mom."

"It's just that I can't believe I did that–in the Crystal Ball Room, in that kind of crowd."

"Well, finish it before Dad comes back in wanting to eat."

"OK." She scooted back out of the booth and spread her hands, palms facing him. "So, there I am in that circle of people I don't know, and I'm making a plan: as soon as there is a break in the discussion, I will make a

short but appropriate remark. And then, I will follow it by saying, 'Have you tried the hors d'oeuvres? I hear they're delicious. I think I'll go check them out.'

"But obviously that's not what happened."

She brought her hands up to her mouth.

"No. When there was a break in the conversation, I said quite crisply and distinctly, 'Oh, I understand that quite well. I'm rather nearfarted myself.'"

Kevin laughed and brought his hands to his knees, staring at her.

"What'd they do?"

"Do? They didn't do anything, just stood there in a sudden silence. They didn't even have eye contact!"

"They probably didn't know whether you were trying to be gross or whether you had a bit too much to drink."

"I hadn't even finished the first glass! Can you imagine? To say FART in polite social conversation? Well, I had to do something. These people might just stand like this all evening."

"I can remember when you gave me a whap with the spatula for saying fart."

"Well, you were in the first grade."

Kevin shrugged.

"How'd you worm your way out of it?"

"Said, 'Oh, have you tried the delicious hors d'oeuvres–think I will.' Then, I got out of there."

Kevin looked up at his mom, shaking his head.

She shook her head back, whirled, went to the sink, took down a glass and filled it with water.

She turned back around.

"Oh, I wouldn't be too concerned," he said. "Being nearfarted is not so bad. It's when you get FARFARTED that you're trouble."

Vedi came back into the kitchen in his robe.

"You two still talking? You better let this boy get some sleep. Want some cereal son?"

God, I will miss having Kevin around.

August 15, Friday, 3:30 PM

She's a choice selection to be the wing supervisor. Margie's whole demeanor evokes a personality in control of her body, detailed to the individual eyebrows brushed upward. She lifts and settles a manicured hand onto the blanket, beside mine, and studies my face a few seconds.

"How would you like to go home for the day tomorrow?"

She's watching the crevices at my eyes for a sign of how the question strikes me. I don't visibly react although my abdomen swirls.

"Tomorrow?" I've been gone from home for three weeks.

"Yes. Leave after ten, return tomorrow night. The team recommends that you go again on Sunday."

My brain races with thoughts of me back home. Am I ready? There's no call button at home, no Annabell.

"If Saturday is too much, cancel Sunday. Day-pass is a trial run. Make note of problems you have to face when home is permanent. It's natural for you to be nervous . . ."

"Nervous? Anxious maybe. I LIVE with a doctor! The problem is fetching me back."

Deliberately, I hold my eyes wide, trying to look lively. This is a surprise.

Margie folds her hands like a nest.

"You'll be back, else your insurance won't pay."

I chuckle. "Don't expect me before bedtime."

"Make your arrangements," she says in a serious tone. "It may not easy, but it will be all right."

Why should she assume I will not feel easy with home?

I think of the house we just left this past February. When Mother came back in from looking at the new townhouse we were moving into, she went straight up the stairway to her room without speaking to me. For eight years, we had lived there in the big Williamsburg house. The kids loved it. Vedi and I were never quite happy in it.

You have been up on your nerves since the bleak sun fought through the steaming woods on the back hill, boiling like a pot of sassafras stew, clearing hour by hour, exposing the naked scarecrow trees, dew shivering on the depressed spindles of shaggy evergreens.

The cereal's combed along with the banana peels down the disposal. The poem's not written for the workshop, the paper not edited, lies frigid white on the desk back there, nagging; yet the beds are made, waiting for night to unlock deep warmth when you can close like a shell; but night is hours away.

You pace the floor in your woolly robe, toes wrapped in fleece, warding off winds that sneak through the edges of the windows. You walk the rooms of a house too large to clean in one day, a hotel where you are the maid with lots of experience and not much commitment. The pay is good.

The poem is begun in bad order. You make another round of coffee, change to jeans and force out into the bitter breath to the mailbox to get the bills, the one letter, envelope typed with your typewriter, fat white envelope you can't open right now. Another rejection slip. The workshop poem hangs wet in the back of your mind.

You'll put on soup, make a cake for the dinner tomorrow, wander the halls, look through the panes, twelve panes in each window of this Williamsburg wonder, gray as your mind., like the uncleared fog. You walk slowly, insides whipping, the wind crackling through the briars down over the hill, where the players on the course whack the ball, lift their arms, get in the cart and disappear past the knoll, taking the gaudy chartreuse and orange to another hole.

You watch through a pane with lines dry as milky slug trails left from November squalls. It seems inappropriate, but something in you wants to get a rag, Windex, and wipe; but you've wiped down through this cold see-through calendar so many times; and the lines hang disjointed on the page. Won't make a soup today.

You hug into your knitted red sweater and try to work up a sweat, start the juices, like you would if you had an apartment on the down side of the Village. There'd be hunger there, but you've made a trade for hardwood floors, shiny as you were last week.

Last summer, you tried all month to read Joyce but the words kept gumming together into a wad too heavy to hold when the kids kept saying beach; and you went, and left the book behind.

You see that tree down by the road. Can't tell if it's half dead or just frozen in crusty clay. You want to run out and hug that tree, feel its razor-edged bark cut into your hand, see if it can draw blood. You want to wrap a blanket around its pathetic trunk. Last fall, it stood like a candle but day by day went out. It stiffens as you stare, and waits for spring.

The smell of chocolate calls you back. The clock chimes three.

You practice a welcome, cover the poem with a dusting cloth, smother it in the scent of Endust, turn toward the fridge, envision piles of whipped icing for the cake.

Saturday, August 16, 10:20 AM

Tree trunks and faces fly away. I can hardly focus. Vedi cuts and accelerates, now passing a yellow Volkswagen. My head is spacey, full, and hot. We bend into McClannahan Street. I am seasick.

"Vedi, do you have to go so fast?"

He answers with a pleasant lilt. "I'm only going the limit. So, we have the whole day alone together since Kent, Karen, and your mother took off for West Virginia."

"Kent left his new puppy for us to baby-sit," he adds, giving me a wary grin. A golden retriever. "and Kitty's happily relegated to a downstairs bedroom."

God, if there should be an accident, I would not be able to climb out. How can traveling by car feel so alien?

"Yeah," I answer, selecting words as if I'm learning a new tongue, "Kent told me when I spoke to him yesterday."

We are swinging left onto Avenham and that van is coming straight at us! "Watch–!"

Vedi slams on the brakes in the middle of the turn. The other car pulls on again, the driver giving us a defiant stare. Vedi completes the turn and proceeds, looking to me then back to the street, his lip set.

"Judy, I had the right of way," he finally says.

What is going on with me? Vedi side-glances again, his brows knitted in thought. "Kevin's out getting some lunch for the three of us. You hungry?" He speaks in a vacant tone.

"OK." A sensation of falling, that's what I'm getting. Am I nuts?

My hand slides along the seat belt and rests on the buckle as we crash into a mist where the fat trees of Avenham Avenue protect the renovated old houses from prying eyes.

I close my mine. Vibrations come up from the tires into my hips. Humming wafts me like a boat. I let go into the gentle rocking.

Faith in the hand that rocks the cradle, rocks like a wave, like a boat on water at night in Turkey on the Bosphorus Strait, sunk into the seat of the small motorboat, zigzagging the channel by the gold of the moon and a lamp on the prow. The sinewy, old man, leather-worn, reared in a village on the banks of the Strait, ferries us across to the opposite shore. We are the passengers of the night, in the palm of the breeze, helpless, no life jackets, only the eye and maneuvering skill of the old fisherman channels us through.

Vedi jostles me backwards over the threshold. The foyer is cool gray light. An assortment of scents greets my nose and arranges themselves around me like a collage, the potpourri from the powder room, onions ripening in a basket in the pantry, the chemical tinge of laundered shirts hung in the closet, the carpet in the great room baked by the sun, and blueberries from the candle on the coffee table. These are MY scents.

A sudden smell of wet dirt accompanied by rough panting and strawberry-blonde paws with floppy ears skids into my lap. A soggy dishrag tongue and cooked-turnips breath slurps at my face.

Vedi grabs his collar and hoists him back, commanding, "Moses, Mosey down!" Kent's pup is only seven months old, but already too much energy and bulk for a small foyer. The paws have left his signature on my knees.

"Is this the welcoming committee?" I ask. Moses licks my knees and fingers, and woofs at my wheelchair as we creep across the floor. He thinks I'm a stranger.

I am parked amidst pools of light that flood through the picture windows. Warmth penetrates my legs. This is my home, the paintings on these walls, the three-piece glass coffee table I carried up from North Carolina, and Turkish rugs I bargained for. Home. I know where everything in this room came from. Kevin is due back with Chinese, Vedi is making iced tea in the coffee maker, and I feel a bit overwhelmed.

The usual, dull aching crawls through my bones. I must ignore it. The sun splits through the coffee table to the carpet. The table is cluttered, books, magazines, the crystal bowl from Poland, and a plant that's thriving under Mother's thumb. My plants do well when she's here. Look at the flowers on the balcony. But the underside of the coffee table is smeared with fingerprints. People forget that the bottom has to be wiped.

Vedi slips up to my side. "Tea will be ready shortly, can I get you anything in the meantime?"

"As a matter of fact, hand me your dishtowel and get me the Windex." He looks a bit startled but he complies.

"What do you think you're doing?" Vedi asks, coming up behind me.

"These should go back on the shelf," I answer.

He lifts the stack of books from my lap and lays them above the television.

"We can do this later," he says gently.

"But everything's out of place. Everything's been moved." A surge for spring-cleaning has come over me, a desire to roll up my sleeves, tie up my hair, and scrub down every corner of this house.

But when I look back at the confusion on my husband's face, waves of my aching, burning, and exhaustion begin their seep back into me. My arms fall onto the sides of my chair.

All right, don't spoil this precious time today.

Later

I push across the rugs into the great room. It's so quiet. The air-conditioner starts its long, breathy sigh. The purpled mountains are smeared in haze. I imagine steam rising from their bellies. Looking around, I wonder what I can do. Kevin cleaned up the kitchen after lunch.

This is the first time I have been alone in weeks.

How could Vedi let it slip his mind that he is on first-call, in charge of the trauma team?

When Kevin left us, he didn't post a phone number where he could be reached, having no idea that fifteen minutes later the phone would ring and his dad would have to charge out the door to the ER.

"I shouldn't be gone long," Vedi called back to me. Like old times.

The grandfather clock walks its wooden clack through the hall all the way up to my knees. I need to DO something! The balcony.

I start toward the sliding door and stop in front of it. The door sill, can't roll these wheels across those rails. My head is pounding.

"NNNnnnn-ruff!"

I jump. Mosey. He is at my side, sweeping the long hair of his tail like a dust broom, scattering the hundreds of silver pin-points floating in the sunlight. After a second he collapses into a heap on the floor, crosses one leg over the other, places his boxy jaw on the top paw, and winks at me before closing his eyes.

Later

Vedi's been gone an hour and half. My muscles and joints begin to scream in separate, throbbing silence. I should lie down. How I would love to ring for a heating pad. A thrust of my wheel and I am startled by a sudden whelp.

"Mosey! Oh my God, your paw. How could I be so careless?"

He scoots into the hallway continuing to cry.

In the kitchen, I find him, tail down, an abused flicker in his eyes. I coax him. "Come on boy."

I extend a hand.

He whines and sways his whole body, declining my offer. Kent's dog, I'm thinking, probably not been hurt by a human before. And, does he think me human, with this steel and vinyl shell, wheels instead of legs?

Finally, he lets me touch his head, and responds by plunging two vigorous legs up onto mine. Taking his big head between my palms, I kiss him while he whines again for pity.

Margie won't believe this. No need to expect Vedi to return my page. That clerk in surgery told me it was a three-car pile-up. He could be in surgery for hours. Where's my peace of the moment that I was going to hold onto?

My chair rumbles as I spin my wheels across the white squares of tile toward the foyer. Mosey gets to the front door before me, his nose pointed at the handle, his tail swinging like a metronome. He is obviously smiling to be let out. I stop, realizing that I definitely can't venture over the threshold.

I turn the lock and pull open the door. Mosey pushes over me and leaps outside. He squats, then flops down in the grass near the sidewalk.

I call, "OK big dummy, get back in here now."

I force a weak whistle through my teeth.

Mosey shakes his head.

"Mosey!"

He stands, pondering, stares off down the street; then, he looks back at me. There is happy defiance in his eyes. My God, the dog realizes I can't restrain him. He darts to the edge of the lawn, stops, then does a bouncy dance—as I yell.

I crane my neck out the door; but all I can see is the edge of the house, a bit of the yard, the street, and the rock wall.

I go from room to room, waiting for the phone to ring, opening the front door, whistling and calling; but no one even walks by the house. Doctor's wife, doctor's wife! I keep thinking. It's my fault as well, I didn't think to ask him if he was on call, the one thing I ALWAYS have to know before I make plans. I keep envisioning Kent's pup side-swiped by a car, lying beside the road injured or dying, no one to help him.

Three hours later

Kent, Mother, and Karen burst into the front door, their laughter spilling ahead of them. I am on the couch under the coverlet, my eyes red and swollen.

"Mom?"

Kent's voice. I pull the cover back and lean up on an elbow. Kent and Karen seem magnified, looking down on me with dumbfounded expressions.

"Where's Dad?" Karen asks.

"Where's Kevin?" Kent is alarmed.

Mother cautiously peers a wind-blown head through the shoulders of the kids. Her arms are full of pocketbook, sweater, and plastic bags that I can see are full of tomatoes and cucumbers that I guess are from Aunt Lou.

Like a child, I explain, bursting into tears again, describe letting the dog out.

"I sometimes can't believe this family," Karen says, handing me a tissue. "Why didn't you just watch TV?"

Kent strides out the front door and whistles twice.

In seconds, Mosey bounds across the front stoop.

Sunday, August 17, 3 PM

He lays me down easy onto our waterbed, like I'm a doll that could break. My blue barges nest on the back of their heels atop the flowered sheet. Above, he pauses, surveying me from head to toe. we can't believe we're along in our own bedroom. The Rehab gave me home-leave again today.

Caprice and mystery plays in Vedi's face as he unbuttons the top of his shirt. Raising his brows in suspense, he tosses the shirt onto the floor with the air of a stripper. I'm laughing silently, twisted onto my arm.

He slips from his loafers, unzips his pants, steps out of them, and tip-toes to the end of the bed, raising his hands like an orchestra conductor.

"Ready, Love?" I turn onto my back and eye him.

"The mind is ready but the body is weak."

"Well, we'll just have to do something about that," he answers, lowering his arms. each hand pops a bow on my shoes, picks apart the strings, curls up each tongue, and deftly slides them off my feet. He lifts each foot separately, balancing an ankle in one hand while pulling my socks off, peeling my feet as if they are delicacies, flinging the limp socks over his shoulders.

He sees my desparing look at the new braces. He puts a finger to his lips. "Shhh," he whispers, tearing back the Velcro straps. "They'll be gone for two hours."

In no time, he climbs in beside me and envelopes us head to toe in sheets. I roll to him. We are tasting each other's pineapple upside-down cake breath.

"Your mother really went out of her way on the dinner today," he says, stroking his finger down my nose, pausing to rub at the nub.

My hand clutches a handful of his fleshy breast.

"Those ripe tomatoes!" I say.

"You can never get your fill of fresh vegetables," he whispers, moving his body to mine.

Wednesday, August 20, 10:30 AM

"I did it! I did it!" My ecstatic squeal leaps above the routine whirs and thumps of Out-Patient, where I stand on my numb legs between parallel bars, my eyes glued to hands lest they lose grip of the steel which holds me up.

"All right!" Annabell cheers from the side.

With childish glee, I want the whole world to see. There should be a video, fireworks, a parade with clowns. With my arms and upper torso, I have just lugged my feet forward for the first two new STEPS of this summer.

Light from the window strikes into the mirror at the end of the bars. My eyes dart into it.

Shimmering Aurora, goddess of the dawn, reborn out of darkness—morning sun, illuminating my reflection.

"One more time!" Annabell calls.

Mentally drawing the light around me, I manage to do it one more time.

And then, I do it again.

Thursday, August 28, 3:30 PM

I watch my biceps rise and fall with the alternate movement of the weights. Annabell's working at her desk. Tomorrow, she is going to teach me to fall with the crutches.

A fortyish blonde-haired woman walks through the door. As she goes to Annabell, I notice how the sleeve of her dress is folded up and pinned at the shoulder.

"No one knows the pain I suffer," the patient tells me.

"Looks like it would be healed."

"Oh, the stump's healed; but, I have pain same as if that car wreck just happened."

"Can't you take medicine?"

"Oh, I've done been addicted to pills by the handfuls that weren't doing me much good anyway."

I try not to stare toward her phantom limb.

Annabell mumbles, pulling the strap down around the woman's uninjured shoulder, showing her the button on the control, which she will push to send electrical current into the stump. They practice turning the juice on and off. The woman claims she can't detect the current. Annabell twists the dial as far as it will go.

"I feel it!"

Seeing my reaction, Annabell explains. "This gadget works on the premise of producing pain that will distract a greater pain—for instance, that in the ghost of a limb."

When the woman is gone, Annabell comes to sit.

"This is one of those low points in my profession. How can you help heal a phantom?"

Thursday, August 29, 3:00 PM

I move toward the open door. Annabell stands near, but I propel myself.

"Let your weight fall into each step. Get balanced before you take another."

A deep breath, and I squeeze the metal frame of the walker and lean heavily, trembling in my biceps and knees, haunted by falling.

"Come on, rally, slough off the fear!"

I lift and clop, stabilize, then raise and slush the metal frame. Halfway across the room ,I see Doctor Nolan. His face is all smiles.

"Miracles," he says quietly.

". . . surprised, pleased–no, amazed by your progress," Don is saying, "Drs. Miller, Godwin and I agree that MS can be ruled out at once and for all."

A veil of relief falls over me.

"We estimate, at present, that the strength in your right leg is seventy percent and the left, forty."

I calculate: Ninety percent still ahead. Nerve endings heal only one-tenth of an inch per week.

"When will I get back to normal?"

"It's hard to predict. You should, however, be prepared to deal with some permanent loss. But with your determination, it's a good prognosis. Just plan to use vehicles for quite some time."

"I feel like a Lazarus."

He nods.

I could add that it's occurred to me that THE Lazarus just might have been raised from a very bad case of GBS.

"Well, you're living proof that a positive attitude aids healing. Jim Miller asked me to tell you that he finds your improvement to be most remarkable."

My soul is refined, returns in its spirals toward peace, life after life. I have not been paralyzed before, nor have I risen from deadened limbs,

*neither waited like a tree, nor spread my leaves in such gratitude nor bent
so low in despair and pain. But, I have passed through this valley. In no
future will this particular trial be mine. I have waded this river in dark
and dusk and dawn. I have not cried why me nor stopped moving with the
flow, though I have pushed and stiffened with the thrust, let go only at the
falls, and learned to receive any grace-filled hands that have deemed to help
pull me from that nameless water at my thighs. It is leaving me a flooded
land. There is much debris to gather.*

Tuesday, September 2, 3:30 PM

I'm on the brink. Stretching forward, I lock my wheels and stare.
It's a LONG way down. But, Annabell's told me that it takes forty
percent more muscle to descend than to ascend.

It looks so deep, no wonder it's called a stairwell.

A week ago, I told Annabell, "I lie in the bed at night and worry about
a fire." Today, she has brought he here to show me a solution. Fourteen
steps down. If I can make it to that last step down there, I can come back.

"Just put your butt in reverse, and scoot back up, one step at a time."

I am impressed.

"This is nothing," she insists, "in big cities, the disabled go up and
down stairs in their wheelchairs by using the strength in their arms."

I am standing. My arms and hands are latched onto the top of the
stairs railing.

Annabell shifts down to the second step in front of me.

"Descending real stairs is more of a challenge than the six portable
steps we've been using for the past week. Concentrate only on the
moment."

My mind gets a jolt from a sudden vision of my body's being
sucked out and helplessly hurled head over heels.

A flight of stairs!

"I'm right in front of you. Don't look down."
I focus on Annabell's shoulders and arms.
"When you tire, sit. This is no contest for speed."
I grin at the word, *speed.*
As she tells me, I turn so that my body is flush with the handrail.
My fingers get a solid grip. I'm getting set to slur my leg over the side
of the first big step. I remind myself that courage is the highest virtue;
and remember Annabell's repeated words:

You will only learn to walk again with the courage to not fear falling.

With meticulous care, I alternately cling to the rail with one sweaty
hand, wipe the other on my shirt, and place it back on the rail.
Holding on–
a climber scaling off a mountain,

I slip a blue barge off the side.

You must want to take that step more than you fear.

My braces are stiff and heavy. For what seems a long while, my leg
hangs stupidly in the air like cargo being lowered onto the deck of a
barge.
Finally, my foot touches concrete. I level my breathing as I shift on
the rail and brace myself. Inch, twist, and I scoot the other foot until it
slides from the rim and plops beside its mate.
"Turn around and see where you've come from!" Annabell's voice
is loud and sparkling.
I'm aching all over, but I'm wobbly with excitement as I inch around.
I had to sit three times coming down; and once I cried; but, I've done it,
I have! Annabell is supporting me now from my back.

There's a rustling above us. My eyes flit back over the steps: My family, shadowed at the top.

How long have they been there watching me?

My ears are full of their voices, echoing down and up again.

I hold on tight, and steady my stance.

As I wait, they will reach me.

*The Fiddler's bow feathers into my senses the clear mountain air, all around me. **I'll fly away, oh glory!** and I breathe in the lightness of **Yes.***

My spirit's caught up—dancing back and forth on the rim of the steps.

AFTERWARDS

November 1990

I am meditating as I walk the road that circles my hill. This is my fifth time around, and my thoughts are coming with me. I can walk two miles a day now—and relish the sound of the yards grinding away under my feet. The crackle of the gravel, spilling back at a constant pace, is my momentary control. The pumping tension and release in the muscles of my legs as they propel me forward at my will, makes me grateful. I never walk this circle without musing on how much has changed for me since the summer of 1985. It took me until the following summer to begin to gain my former strength. Now, I have only mild disability in my left foot and my knees.

Karen is scouting for a college next year. Kevin is in Massachusetts, working on a thesis in writing and English, and doing an apprenticeship with a publisher. Kent is back from a year in Turkey, where he got a masters degree in history. Vedi comes and goes from the hospital, making rounds, doing surgery. I continue with my work. And, oh yes, Rebekah, others and I did bring forth the Blue Ridge Writers Conference that fall. It was a great success. Also, that fall, I was out with my wheelchair and crutches teaching my night classes.

GBS taught me: To live in the present; to be grateful; that the only real control we have is now; that the power of the Spirit is phenomenal; and that we are everything we have known.

October 2000

Now, I can stay up half the night writing, sleep late, and go out and walk four miles. Vedi is retired. The children have found their own lives. Karen, Pete's wife, Cathy, and I nursed Mother here in my home for seven months before she died of cancer five years ago at age eighty-one. She died with the same quiet reserve of strength and dignity that she demonstrated throughout her life. Vedi's mother died in her sleep six years ago at age ninety-four. Vedi has completed his project of the past three years with Turkey, as an international health care consultant for the hospital system where I spent the six weeks of rehabilitation in 1985. We look forward to fun with family, travel, seminars, writing, and painting–one step at a time.

When life passed from Mother, she seemed to have fallen asleep, her head a bit to the right, a tired face that immediately took on a gray pallor. I straightened her head, lowered her bed to a comfortable level, pulled the covers up, and placed her arms across her abdomen, one pale hand over the other. At last, her whole body was numb–as were her feet and hands these last months–a body spent and exhausted.

I lit a large rose candle and sat for a long time in the flickering light with her to comfort her spirit lest it be confused. I think Granny and Grampaw met her coming and welcomed her over there. She went to the cabin in the woods she often wished about, in a meadow full of wild flowers. I know she dreams me well.

In that log cabin is cooking mustard greens, the lid dancing a jig on hot bubbles; and deviled eggs sit in an ice box, nesting. Outside, beyond the wide porch with the two cane rockers, is a field of flaxen grasses swaying in the warm air that moves like a giant hand of a goddess to bless Mother as she comes down the steps, young as she used to be here when I was a girl.

She is full of sunshine and Glad again. She walks out a stone walk laced with rich dirt and violets at the border. She is wearing blue.

Later, she will go to the sweet spring and draw up cold water in a tin ladle and offer it to Aunt Lou, who brought a peach cobbler, which Uncle Frank and Mother can eat now to their heart's desires.

They play croquet until the sun goes down; then, they wait for the embers in the fireplace to die another time; for tomorrow, they will go over to visit their Mom and Dad, who are always either raising marigolds and hollyhocks or digging up fat potatoes. They all take walks and sing the old songs. There's so many more to visit. They are always waiting for a reunion because it keeps getting bigger and bigger over there while it gets smaller here.

They are patient, knowing the truth of waiting at last; and Mother hardly has time to worry any more about us—because what can happen to us, but that the worst is we should die and come to see her?

Her freckles have blossomed now, rich as her garden, and she walks the hills behind the cabin and picks blueberries and beechnuts, and has fine teeth to chew them up. She remembers only what she doesn't want to forget, as if it were a dream.

Gladys pulls the afghan of the night sky down and tucks it in around her feet and feels at home and wanted in the place she built with her daydreams here—when she never could save up enough for a down payment to have it.

She's told daddy to call before he comes; and she won't see him if she doesn't feel like it, and never on Sundays; and she always gets to be in control of the conversations, and he is not allowed to smoke in her presence.

But she takes time to fish with him and they love watching baseball now together—watch it played down here some Fridays, but not too often.